MY DANISH PASTRY

Lived by
Richard Swindells

and

written by
Guru OM

Guru Om asserts the moral right to be identified as the Author of this work.

©GURU OM 2020

Published by Three Little Birds Press

www.threelittlebirdspress.com

PROLOGUE

It was the end of 1971 and I was 22 years old. Shearing had come to an end for another season. I was still getting tear-stained letters from my mother which were designed to invoke emotional blackmail in me.

I had made quite a bit of money shearing so I decided to go back to England for a short holiday. My thinking was that I would somehow like to create a relationship with my mother that would be based on two adults communicating with each other rather than her treating me as a teenager which she did, in her letters.

I had only been back at her house for a couple of days when a few school chums I knew knocked on the door. After a few minutes of conversation, they invited me to go out drinking with them at one of the local pubs that evening.

After they left my mother said "Who was that then?"
"A few old school chums" I said "They've invited me to go out for a few beers with them tonight."
"Well, don't think you're coming home here drunk like your father did, I had enough of that, living with him!"

The day went on with my step-father Jim sitting in his rocker and my mother fussing around the house.

My sister, Sandra, and I laughed and joked around with each other. The time came for me to get ready to go out or I'd be late. I threw on some good clothes just in time for the knock on the door.

"See ya later everybody." I said in a cheery voice and walked toward the door.

"What time are you coming home tonight Richard? We go to bed at 11 o'clock here so if you're not home by then the house will be locked."

"Suit yaself!" I said as I threw the keys on the table. Now I was really pissed off and angry. Once I got outside with my couple of school chums, who I hadn't seen for years, since I'd left to go to Australia. I put the domestic garbage of mi mothers house aside and went off for a good night out.

It was great being with my two pals and their wives, although I felt a bit left out because everyone I met was married with children. Not that they put any crap on me, they were generous to the max and asked me all about my time in Australia.

That evening we drank a lot of beer at the Star Hotel in Upper Sowerby Bridge. I met a bloke, John Lodge, who I'd been somewhat 'pally' with at Ryburn School. He was a very short bloke and like most short men he had a complex about it! A real chip on his shoulders!

As the night went on, he got into some trouble with three blokes from another area. So, muggins me, thinking that I was still in Australia where mates are real mates, walked over to where they were standing at the bar. The three blokes were threatening to punch his head in, so I said "Ya having problems Johnny?"

"Yeah Dick, these three blokes are hassling me."

"Leave him alone fellas. He's not on his own now, there's two of us!"

"Great!" said one bloke, then hauled off and punched me in the face. I shook my head and said "Good shot mate! Now its my turn." I cracked him in the head with a big right hand and arse over head he went, but next minute found me on the floor with two of his mates on top of me. All I remember was rolling around the barroom floor and under the round tables. There were punches flying everywhere and most of them were aimed at me!

Out of the corner of my eye I saw John lodge crawling away, under the tables and out of harms way.

"Hey! Where are you sneaking off to Johnny?" I called. He never looked back. Once he was away from the fight he kept going. Straight out the door!

When it was finally over, I was in a right mess. Although the three blokes had various injuries, I'd caught a few punches myself, mainly in the face. Steve and Colin helped me clean myself up a bit but nothing could repair my shirt that was covered in blood, with a big tear down the front.

I walked home alone that evening vowing to myself not to help anyone else when it wasn't my problem. My bigheartedness and sense of loyalty had yielded me a fat lip, bloodied nose and a bruised cheek. 'Iris is not going to like this.' I thought. As I walked down the cobblestone street towards her house.

When I tried the door, it was locked and the lights were out. It was about 1.30am and there was a thick layer of frost covering the house walls. I started to feel the cold now as I was only wearing a thin shirt and a cardigan. It was obvious to me that she would blow her brains out if I knocked at this time so I decided to look for some shelter or another way into her house. I tried the lower window but it was firmly locked. The cellar coal chute was wet and black from coal dust, so that was out of the question. The only other option I could see was to sit on the outside toilet until the morning and do the best I could to keep myself from freezing to death.

By about 4 o'clock my false teeth were chattering so badly they were keeping me awake so I took them out and put them in my pocket. It was one of the longest and most uncomfortable nights I think I've ever had. The temperature was below zero but somehow, I managed to make it.

The back door opened at 7 when Jim Bailey came out for the milk. It took me a few minutes to get the stiffness out of my joints. I walked into the house as if nothing mattered at all.

When mi mother saw me, she hit the roof! I was in no mood for one of her lectures so I walked off upstairs to was up and change mi clothes. Once I was cleaned up, I felt a lot better so I lay down on my bed for a few minutes and before long the daydream dissolved into darkness.

I woke up a few hours later, washed mi face, combed mi hair and went downstairs. When I walked into the kitchen, my suitcase was sitting next

to the back door;
"Who put mi suitcase there?"
"I did." Said Jim Bailey.
"What for?"
"Because you're leaving."

FINDING A PLACE TO LIVE ON MY OWN

The decision to say in England for a while meant that I needed somewhere to live, seeing that my own father, mother and stepfather had thrown me out. I had been my own boss in the Outback from the age of 15. Anybody trying to tell me what to do was completely out of the question. Shearing in England, Scotland and Wales was seasonal. Once I ran low on money, I had to get serious about finding work. Asking around my old school chums, it was suggested that I try to get work at a placed called Sagar Richards Aluminum Bronze Foundry. Once the five-minute interview was over, I was hired on the spot. The work consisted of moulding sincro-mesh rings and selector forks for car gearboxes and many other spare parts for all kinds of machinery

Although the work was hard it was nothing compared to shearing and many other jobs I had turned my hand to in the Bush. One of the major influences that caused me to stay in a shit-hole country like England was GIRLS! In the Bush sheep outnumbered girls by a massive amount and in this country, girls were in plentiful supply. Up until this point I had been living at my old school chums house who was married with two children. It was only temporary until something more appropriate came along.

It didn't take very long for me to build up a goodly amount of money and as soon as I had enough behind me to rent something on my own, house-hunting was on the top of my agenda. In Sowerby Bridge Village, I came across a sign that read, Singletons Real Estate and Rentals. After reading what was on offer in the window, I made my grand entrance.

"Good morning." said Mr. Singleton. "Can I help you?"

"G'day, how are ya? I'm looking for something reasonable to rent."

"Where are you from, if you don't mind me asking? You're obviously not from around these parts."

Rather than go into a long dialogue about my accent, I simply said, "Australia."

"How interesting. We don't get many people from Australia around Sowerby Bridge."

"No, I wouldn't think so."

"Are you looking for long-term or short term?"

"Probably about a year or so."

"Oh good. That gives me more of an idea what to look on the books for. Is it just for you or do you have a family?"

"Nope, no family. Just for me."

"Good, that narrows it down a bit. So, can I assume a one-bedroom will be enough?"

"Sounds good to me mate."

After going through his books, he offered me three apartments in different locations. "No thanks mate. Apartments are like rat-boxes to me. Don't you have anything other than that to offer?"

Mr. Singleton scoured his books again and after a few minutes he said, "I've got an interesting old place up Sowerby New Road. It's a one-up, one-down miners' cottage. Now, there are a few things about it you may not like such as it's only got an outside toilet. Would that bother you?"

"Not in the least. If you knew some of the places I've lived in you'd know why."

"All right, that's good. It only has a coal-burning old-fashioned fireplace but there is a gas pipeline that runs down the side of the pavement so it wouldn't cost a great deal to run the service to the downstairs room."

"No worries there mate."

"Now, lastly, and this may be a sticking point, it's only going to be available for 5 years and then we're going to pull it down."

"Why's that?"

"Well it's condemned, due to the fact that they're planning on widening the road in that area."

"No worries mate. I won't need it for that long."

"Well good. Now there is a big plus with this place. You can actually buy it on rental-purchase if you wanted to."

"What does that mean?"

"The owners want 200 pounds for it and if you put 30 pounds down for a deposit and pay 2 pounds a week rent, you'd own it outright after about a year and a half."

"Jesus mate, that sounds like a piss-cutter."

"I beg your pardon?"

"Oh, excuse me mate. What I meant to say was, it all sounds good to me."

"Oh, very good. So, when would you like to inspect the property?"

"How about now? Would that be all right?"

"Not a problem sir. I'll get the key for you."
After Mr. Singleton found the key and gave me
directions to the cottage, I took off walking up
Sowerby New Road. It didn't take long to find the
miners cottage as it was right where the Estate
Agent said it would be.

There was a big downside to the house. Directly
across from Cavendish Buildings was Boston Street
which was the street my mother lived on. Talk about
luck, and I don't mean good luck! Running off of
Sowerby New Road was a cobblestone passage
about four feet wide with three steps at the end,
which led to four old miners' cottages joined
together. Number 8 was the third cottage along.
Opening the door of Number 8 revealed quite a large
room with stone slab floors. There was a fireplace
on the right-hand side. On the far right-hand side
was an old stone sink that was about 2 inches deep.
The sash window was on the right side of the door
and opposite the door was another door that led up
to the one bedroom. The bedroom was, as I expected
it to be, one large room. What I didn't expect was
another door that led up to an attic. The attic could
have been another bedroom except for the fact that
the roof must have been leaking for years. The thick
plaster that covered the walls was now at the bottom
of the wall in large piles. 'Oh well. no problem
there', I thought, 'as the place is only for me, no one
will be using this room.'

After going back downstairs and surveying the room
for a while, I decided the cottage had enough
potential to make it livable for me. Plus, the fact that

I would have my own roof over my head which meant no more mother telling me what time to be home of an evening and no more sleeping on the outside toilet in subzero temperatures.

Back at Singletons office, I paid the 30 pound deposit and took charge of the keys to the first property that I'd bought. After leaving the Estate Agents office, I caught a double-decker bus back to what was to be my new home. Straight across from Cavendish Building was quite a large corner store which carried just about everything I would need food-wise to keep me alive. I was now short on tobacco so I decided to go in and check it out.

"Can I help you?" said a bald, fat bloke in a broad Yorkshire accent.

"Yeah sport, what kind of rolling tobacco do you have?"

"Sun Valley and Old Holburn sir."

"Which is the strongest mate?"

"I'm not a smoker myself but according to my customers, Old Holburn seems to be. It's my best seller."

"All right, give us 2 ounces and a packet of papers."

"If you don't mind me asking sir, are you Iris' lad that just come over from Australia for a holiday?"

"Yeah mate. That's me."

"Oh I know your mother really well. She's been a good customer of mine since she's lived in Boston Street."

"Well that's good." I said.

"Are you staying long?"

"I'm not sure yet mate. I just bought that old place across the street."

"Well, that's lovely isn't it. You must have done really well in Australia then?"

"Oh yeah, I did. I'm well-known and wealthy, just like you." This little joke of mine threw him for a loop. He didn't know what to say in return so I said, "Just bull-shittin' ya' mate." which caused his eyebrows to raise up so far they joined his receding hairline. "Good on ya mate." I said as I made mi way out of his shop. "See ya around."

"Yes sir." he said. "Thank you for coming in."

"No worries mate."

MEETING MI MUM ON THE STREET

Back out on the street, I waited for a few cars to pass. As I stood there, mi mother walked around the corner.

"How are ya?" I said as she almost bumped into me.

"Oh, I never saw you there! You made me jump. What are you doing around here? I thought you were living at ya boozing pals house?"

"No mother, not anymore. You'll be happy to know I'm your new neighbor."

"What do you mean by that?"

"I bought that house across the street. Number 8 Cavendish Buildings."

"Are you kidding me?" she said with a look of horror on her face.

"No mother. I couldn't stand being too far away from you."

"That's a likely bloody story. I'll bet you bought that on bloody purpose just to embarrass me and show me up in front of mi neighbors."

"In spite of what you think, not everything I do in my life is about you."

"Ya father won't be too pleased when I tell him."

"I take it you mean your husband? What business would it be of his?"

"The further away you live from us, the better we like it. I suppose you'll be stumbling home drunk every night, making a bloody fool out of yourself in front of the whole street?"

"I don't think your friends will be up at 2 o'clock in the morning, waiting for me to 'stumble home

7

drunk', as you put it."

"I wish to bloody hell I had never let you go to Australia in the first place!" she said, as she turned around abruptly and went into the corner store.

"Hey Steve." I said as I walked into mi mate's house. "I just bought miself an old cottage down Sowerby New Road so I'll be out a' ya' hair in a couple of days mate."

"Oh ya' not in our hair Dick Lad but I'm real happy ya' found a place of ya' own. What ya' gonna' do for furniture and bedding? You've got nought."

"That's no problem Steve. I'll go to a second-hand joint to get what I need and they can deliver it for me."

"Well what about bedding and a mattress? We've got plenty of spare blankets and stuff you can borrow till ya get yaself set up mate."

"That's really kind of ya' Steve. I'll only need 'em for a week or so till I can get mi own."

"No problem Dick Lad. I'll get the missus to dig 'em out, once she gets home. Ya' don't have to rush ya know. We've enjoyed havin' ya here. It's been a lot of fun."

Back at mi old cottage found me sat on the cold slab floor surveying the big, high ceilinged room, contemplating what I was going to do with it to make it comfortable. First up, the fireplace had to go. Dealing with shoveling coal on to it would be too much of a problem in cold weather as the coal cellar was outside. Wallpaper would be needed on the walls as the existing paper was dirty and hanging off in places. The stone sink was all of 2 inches deep. That definitely had to go and be replaced with a sink unit and new taps. There was no stove to cook on so a second-hand gas stove would be required. The room was so large that with a few 4 x 2 lengths of wood and some 8' x 4' plywood, I decided a room divider with a serving hatch was on the menu. Last but not least, a wall to wall carpet!

INVITING MI MUM FOR A CUPPA TEA

After a month, the cottage had been completed to
my satisfaction and was very comfortable. I decided
to walk across the street, to where my mother lived,
and invite her to my place for a good, old-fashioned
cup of tea. To my astonishment, she accepted my
offer.

In the couple of years I lived in England, before
returning to the Bush in Australia, I did everything
within my power to create, at least, a warm friendly
relationship with my mother. No matter what I said
or did, it was doomed before it started. Sitting on my
new second-hand couch, drinking a cup of hot tea,
she looked around the room at all the work I had
done.

"So, how do you like it Mother?" I asked.

"I suppose it's not too bad."

"Look at mi new gas fire. She's a beaut don't ya
think?"

"Oh aye. I suppose it will do the job."

"Ya like the wallpaper?"

"Well, I don't. It's not my style but if you like it then
why ask me? You're the one who has to sit here and
look at it."

"I think it's colorful and not too hard on the eyes."

"Why would that matter? You'll probably be too
drunk most of the time to see it."

No matter what I said, the short time she was
visiting always ended up on the negative side. Even
the cup of tea was too strong for her liking! It didn't

take long for her to finish the tea and say, "I think I'll be off; I've got things to do in my place. I've got to make the tea for ya dad."

"No worries." I said, "Thanks for visiting. You're my first visitor." I thought that the fact that she was my first visitor would have pleased her. As my 'real' dad used to say, 'There's no pleasing that bloody wench, no matter what the hell a man does.'

Once she had her coat on and adjusted her hat, I opened the door for her and as she stepped over the threshold I said, "So you like the old place eh?"

"Aye, I suppose it's good enough to bring ya whores back to, along with ya drunken chums."

Although I never responded to her insult, I did think to myself, 'That's it! You selfish, mean-spirited old bitch! That's the last fucking time I invite you to my place!'

OUT WITH MI MATES

For the next few weeks, my spare time was spent going out evenings with some of my old school chums I had reconnected with. We had great times, over a few beers, re-hashing some of the antics we used to get up to in our old school days. There was no lack of pubs and clubs to frequent. Sowerby Bridge, itself, had at least ten pubs and four working-men's clubs. Whilst I had been in the Outback shearing sheep and doing various other hard jobs, my school pals had pretty easy jobs working in factories or as drivers' mates for trucking companies.

They also grew up in the Beatles and Rolling Stones era which meant they were very 'trendy dressers'.

One of my mates, Colin Burbidge had said to me when I first got back, "Hey Dick Lad, about ya clothes mate."

"What's wrong with 'em." I asked.

"What's right with 'em!" he said. "You're about 10 years out-a-date. Ya need to grow ya hair long, for a start, if ya wanna' pick up chicks. That straight back and sides haircut of yours isn't gonna' help ya to pull birds. That Italian suit of yours needs to go to Vinnie de Pauls and those business shirts need to be used as window cleaning rags."

I hadn't given my clothes much of a thought as everyone in the Bush dressed the same way I dressed. Anyone who had slightly long hair would have been labeled a 'faggot'. It didn't take me long to catch on to my new surroundings so these days, my hair was starting to grow over my ears and I wore the latest fashionable clothes that were available in Halifax.

One particular evening, around 8, a couple of my old mates came down from Beachwood Housing Estates to visit me. Beachwood was a well-known housing estate in the small village of Sowerby which could be found at the end of Sowerby New Road.
"Hey Dick Lad, how ya going mate? We just called in to see if ya wanna' come for a few beers with us."
"Come in." I said as they stood on the door step grinning from ear to ear.
Once inside, I showed 'em around mi new place which didn't take more than a couple of minutes as there was only 2 livable rooms.
"Fuckin' hell Dick Lad! What a great little pad you've got here. I wish I had a place like this. I'm still livin' at mi mothers' house and she won't let me bring any birds home which is a bloody drag."
"So where ya off to for a few beers?" I asked.
"Sowerby Bride mate. There's a pub at the end of the street that's got a disco on and they've also got a one-man band called Eddie George."
"What do ya mean, 'One-man band'?"
"He plays old rock and roll numbers from the 50's. He's got two big column speakers, an amp, guitar and a drum machine. For one man, he's pretty good."
"Are there gonna' be any sheilas there?" I asked.
"What the hell are 'Sheilas'?"
"Sorry mate, I forgot where I was living. Birds, women, chicks?"

"Course there are mate. Why d'ya think we're going!"

"Alright. Give us a couple of minutes to chuck on some good gear and I'll be right with ya."

"Hey Dick Lad, you're gonna' have to learn to speak English again if ya plan on staying around here. The chicks will think you're some kind of a fancy, white wog (west oriental gentleman) with an accent like yours!"

"Yeah, I know mate. Someone at work already asked me if I was a poofta on account of my accent." I said.

Once I had mi good gear on, we hauled off down the road for a night out on the town. With a pint a-piece of Websters' Bitter in our hands, we found a table and chairs against the wall of quite a large disco room. Eddie George, which was a stage name, had all of his one-man band gear set up center stage but the man, himself, was nowhere to be seen.

Most of the people, on the dance floor, were girls dancing with each other, whilst their ugly girlfriends were sat at the table guarding their handbags. As soon as the DJ stopped the records spinning, there was a 5-minute break before the one-man show started.

"Here he comes!" said one of mi chums. "That's Eddie George." I had expected to see a slim bloke with a 50's style haircut, slicked back with Brylcream, leather jacket and tight trousers. Instead, a fat bloke with a regular short, back and sides haircut walked out. He had a cheap-looking shirt, baggy jeans that his gut hung out of and a pair of regular old baseball boots.

"Jesus Christ." I said. "Who the fuck is this bastard?

14

Ya sure this is the right bloke?"

"Yeah Dick Lad. That's him. That's the one-and-only Eddie George!"

As he tuned up his guitar, I said "Are ya sure this bloke can play?"

"Yeah Dick Lad. He's not too bad. He's no Buddy Holly but he does a half-decent job." Once he was satisfied that his guitar was in tune, he launched into his first song, 'Peggy Sue'. The fat man was not too bad at all. He had the vocals going through an echo machine along with the guitar. The drum machine never missed a beat as it pounded out a rock and roll tempo. Half way through his set, he removed his shirt and was left standing there with a grey-ish white T-shirt on. The only problem with that move was his big, beer-belly and 'man-boobs' that jiggled around when he danced at the chorus of each song. In between songs, he spoke to the audience a bit and told a couple of good jokes.

"What d'ya think Dick Lad? Ya think he's any good?"

"Yeah mate, apart from him being a fat fuck, I like him but why aren't the girls dancing?"

"They generally don't dance to his music. They take a break and have a smoke and a drink. Soon as the disco comes back on they'll be up on the dance floor again."

"Why aren't there any blokes up on the floor?" I asked.

"They're like me mate. They're too scared. They usually get up a half an hour before closing time when they're pretty drunk. That way, if they make fools out of themselves, who cares!"

After Eddie George had finished his show, he and

15

his girlfriend started to roll up cables and dismantle mic stands and the speakers.

"Back in a minute." I said to my mates. "I'm just off to have a chat to the act."

"G'day mate." I said to Eddie as he was rolling up another cable. "Good show mate."

"Ow do." said Eddie. "Glad ya liked it. Mi voice was a bit off tonight as I've done 3 gigs this week."

"Well, it sounded alright to me mate." I said.

"Thanks for saying so lad. I don't get much appreciation at this place but still it's a gig and they pay alright. Where are you from lad? Ya not from around these parts with an accent like that are ya?"

"Originally I am but I've been living in the Outback of Australia since I was a boy."

"I knew ya wasn't from around here lad. I thought maybe ya come up North from London."

"Where else do ya play besides this place?"

"Oh, all over, Lad. I'm playing at West End Club on weekend, Saturday night. Why don't ya come along? It's always grand to have someone who appreciates me."

"Yeah, I just might do that Eddie. Do ya ever let anyone sit in with ya?"

"Sometimes I do. Why, what d'ya play?"

"Trumpet and guitar but I've only got the trumpet at the moment. I'm gonna' get a guitar and amp once I've got a few bob."

"What style of music do you play on the horn?"

"Oh blues, trad and some main-stream stuff."

"Have ya been playing long?"

"Since I was seven."

"That long eh? I suppose ya play pretty good?"

"Yeah, I'm not too bad at all."

"Can ya play Tom Jones type stuff?"

"I sure can mate. I can play anything that has a good melody line with it."

"Right then. Well why don't ya show up on Saturday night and we'll see how ya go." Last orders had been called some time back so we caught the last double-decker back up Sowerby New Road. In those days, not many people had cars so the last bus home was always full of rowdy drunks and tonight was no exception. Back home, in mi old cottage, I was sat on mi second-hand, black, fake leather chair with red, crushed velvet cushions. The gas fire was going full-bore as the English weather was now starting to turn really cold. Some of the blokes that I worked with at the Foundry said they would not be surprised to see it snow earlier than usual this year. Although I lived most of my boyhood years on the bleak Penine moor, I was not looking forward to snow or sleet of any description.

5

SELF INQUIRY

Sitting there in front of the gas fire, staring into the flames that heated up the four burners, I started to contemplate how life had brought me back to, what I considered to be, a shit-hole country. I had avoided buying a television as I had already seen most of mi mates that I had visited in the first couple of weeks that I'd been back, sat in front of the TV, half-drunk in a vegetated state, rotting away, whilst still in the their 20's. The wallpaper around the fire was fake brick-work. No distraction there. 'How the fuck does life determine where one lives or travels?' I asked miself. Most people who lived around these parts had only traveled as far as Blackpool which was a seaside holiday place a couple of hours drive away. My mind traveled, back in time, to all the wonderful adventures I'd had in the Bush, War Dog, Freddie, Ivers, Gundy and all the rest of mi shearing mates. They were probably still sat at Gilltraps bar spinning out the endless bullshit that we knew as entertainment. After dwelling on Lake Cargelligo for a while, my mind latched onto mi mother, who was now a stone's throw away, which didn't please me at all. Had I have been able to find a place to live, miles away from her and her fat old husband, I would have done but again, life had stuck me here.

Ever since I was a small boy, I loved being on my own. I was very familiar with talking to myself and depending on what the inner subject matter was about; I had no problem answering myself out loud.

Sometimes, just to make a point, I had figured out over the past few months that one of the reasons I was back here was obviously my mother. My relationship with my mother was intense and violent.

My mind wandered back to the early 50's, then jumped forwards to the early 60's. Backwards and forwards it wandered as I sat there doing my best not to get emotionally involved with it as it threw up a ton of bullshit for me to deal with. Deep, deep down, in the depth of my heart, it was obvious to me how much I loved my mother. The problem was, she refused to let the mother-son relationship evolve into a best friend relationship which I now required, if I was to have any relationship with her at all. Here I am, in my 20's and here she is, still trying to tell me what to do and how to behave. Guilt. That's what it was. Plain and simple, unadulterated fucking guilt. That's what had dragged me back here. Also, the false idea that she would recognize me as a grown man. Once I accepted this little discovery, I was really fucking angry! Fucking guilt, I thought. If guilt is such a powerful emotion that it can drag me 12,000 miles back to my childhood village, then I really need to figure out what I'm feeling guilty about.

Many movies flooded my mind as I sat there puffing on a smoke. It became, all too apparent, that no matter what I tried to do with the basic mother-son relationship, other than my dropping dead, nothing was going to change my mother into the mother I would have liked to have. From her viewpoint, nothing was going to change me into the 'poofta' son that she desired. Whatever my mother required of me, in my mind, meant squashing myself, as in no drinking, smoking or wearing long hair. That's not all, I would have to become like David fucking Horsefall, who was the son of mi mothers next door neighbor. 'Saint fucking David.' I thought.' The fucking shirt-lifter that could do no wrong in mi mother's eyes.' I couldn't fucking live with miself if I looked and acted like him. Me becoming like that was out of the fucking question. In those days, Mick Jagger was a rock god. Eric Clapton, Peter Townsend, Jimmy Page. Had mi mother wanted me to be like any of them, I would have gladly accommodated her. The bottom line was, I could never be myself as I am in my mother's company. Her non-acceptance of me followed me through life for a good many years.

Here am I, sitting here, the same ignorant piece of shit that no one likes because I won't change into something acceptable that can be placed in a fucking pigeon hole. From that day, henceforth, my promise to myself was, never to compare myself to anyone else. To destroy every bit of societies programming I found within myself until I was left with what I started out with. I am now deprogrammed and dangerous, from the standpoint of an ignorant man. I love myself in spite of everything not because of anything. My simple child-like state is now acceptable. My Natural State!

I had been sitting in front of the fire for a couple of hours now. It was getting quite late so I decided to go to bed and pick up later on where I had finished off in my self-inquiry.

6

INVITING MI DAD TO THE CLUB

Saturday night soon rolled around. I decided to visit mi dad to see if he wanted to go to the West End Club and watch me perform.

"What are you bloody doing here?" he said as he opened his front door in nothing but his long johns and shirt.

"G'day dad, how are ya?"

"I'm alright. Well, don't just stand there on the bloody door-step lad. Come in, it's freezing bloody cold out there." Inside mi dad's 3-bedroom terraced house it was lovely and warm as he had a well-stocked coal fire roaring away in the fireplace.

"Take ya coat off then and sling it over the chair and pull that other armchair up in front of the fire." Although mi dad was not the best of housekeepers, his front room was set up to support his needs as he was quite an old man now. The door to his room had a home-made cloth sausage rolled up and placed at the bottom of his door to stop any drafts blowing in. He had made himself a double-wide platform with his mattress and blankets on it which he had placed in the corner.

"So ya sleeping in the front room now, are ya dad?"

"Damn right I am lad. This cold, bloody weather is playing havoc with mi rheumatism. As warm as this room is, I've still got to rub mi bloody legs to get the circulation going." Mi dad was born in 1897. He was 75 years old at the time. In all those years, apart from a few aches and pains, he'd never had a day's sickness in his life. He had lied about his age and joined the Army, voluntarily, when he was 16, as all the boys on his street had gone to war and he didn't want to be left as the only boy with a bunch of girls. He was a survivor of Word War 1 trench warfare. He'd been mustard-gassed twice and had dysentery 3 times and he'd been shot in the arm with a machine-gun bullet. The horrors he had seen in those trenches, as a young boy, colored his outlook on life. "Ya want me to make ya a pint-pot of tea dad?" "Aye, that would be bloody good lad. Just make sure ya make it strong. I can't stand tea that looks and tastes like piss!" What mi dad meant by this was, 2 heaping teaspoons of Brook Bonds tea leaves in the bottom of a porcelain pint mug with scalding hot water poured over the top.

As a boy, I had watched him drink his tea this way for years. I couldn't understand how all the tea leaves floating on the top did not bother him. As I was waiting in his cold kitchen for the water to boil, I lifted up the lid of his big saucepan that was sitting on one of the spare gas rings. To my surprise, a cooked pigs head stared out at me. It still had eyes in its head and looked like it had a big grin on its face. 'Jesus!', I thought to miself. 'How can he eat things like that?' The water had now come to a boil so I poured it over the tea leaves in the bottom of his mug which caused the leaves to swirl around and finally settle on the top of the hot water. Again, I thought to myself, 'How can he drink tea like that?' Sometimes he would have his tea with milk and sugar. I yelled out to him "Ya want milk and sugar in it?"
"Aye, stick some milk in it and a tablespoon of

sugar." Once the milk and sugar were added, I stirred it around and watched more tea leaves float to the surface. I did my best to scoop some of the leaves out but the more I scooped them out, the more the leaves that rested on the bottom of the mug floated to the surface. 'Fuck this for a joke.' I thought. 'This will have to do!' The tea had now steeped and was a really dark brown color. It looked to me like strong coffee!

"Here ya go dad. I trust it's to your liking." I handed him his mug and he took a small sip of it and said, "It's a bit bloody weak but I suppose it will do."

"Did ya win anything on the horses this week dad?"

"No, not a bloody thing. I think I broke even which is better than bloody losing, I suppose. I won 120 quid about 3 weeks ago. I had a Trifecta come in so I was right pleased about that."

"What did you do with the money? Gamble it back?"

"Not on your bloody nelly lad. I stuck it under mi mattress with the rest of mi money."

"So what ya gonna do with it all?"

"I'm gonna by miself a couple of double-breasted tailor-made suits and as soon as summer rolls around again, I'm off back to Whitley Bay for a couple of weeks holiday."

"Ya like that seaside resort eh?"

"I'ye, it's a grand place. It's nice and quiet and it's got a lot of good pubs. The beers a lot better than it is around here too."

"Hey dad, I'm off to the West End Club tonight. Ya feel like coming out for a few beers."

"What the bloody hell are ya going there for? It's an

old codgers club."

"I met this bloke, Eddie George, the other night in one of the pubs in Sowerby bridge. He's got a one-man band and he's playing there. He says I can play the trumpet with him for a few numbers. I thought I'd take him up on it."

"Well, I wasn't gonna' go out tonight. The weather's supposed to be really bloody cold but I suppose If I wrap up well I'll be alright. Mi old mate Gavin will be there, I could have a couple of pints and a natter to him seeing as I haven't seen him for a few weeks."

"So you'll come?"

"Aye. I don't see why not. It'll make a change from sitting in front of mi tele all night."

"Good on ya dad. If we get there about 7, that will give me time to go home and grab the trumpet and you can sit in the club and have a pint. Does that sound alright to you?"

"Aye, that'll give me time to have a wash and get ready. Are ya still living at ya bloody mothers place?"

"No, I'm buying a cheap one-up, one-down cottage on rental purchase. She threw me out 'cause I wouldn't stop drinking."

"Is she still living with that big, fat nancy boy, Jim Bailey?"

"Yeah, she's still with him."

"That doesn't surprise me. If anybody deserved each other, it's those two buggers!"

"Ya still don't like her, after all these years dad?"

"Like her? I lived with that wench for 12 long years lad. In all that time, all she could do was nag, nag, nag. That's all that bloody wench was good for.

Never bloody satisfied. Didn't matter what the hell I did for her, it was never bloody good enough. Like her? If the old cow dropped dead on the spot, I wouldn't bat a bloody eyelid! As far as I'm concerned, she can rollox her tot! The pair of 'em can go to hell, which is where they belong!"

After mi dad was washed and dressed up in his good tailor-made suit, we caught the double-decker at Kenworthy lane. Our destination was the West End Club which mi dad was a member of.
"Why don't you go straight in the club dad. I'll run off home to my place and get the trumpet."
"Aye, alright then. I'll go grab a pint and look for mi old mate Gavin." It didn't take long before I was back at the club with mi trumpet in hand.
"Hello young fella." said the doorman. "Are you a member?"
"No, but mi dad is."
"Is he in the club now?"
"Yeah."
"What's his name?" he asked me.
"George Swindells."
"Oh alright then. You're George's lad are ya?"
"I sure am."
"Well, normally I'd have to go fetch him to sign ya in but I've known ya dad for years. I'll sign ya in miself. That'll save him coming out a' club room."
On the way past the bar, I got miself a pint of Websters Best Bitter and made mi way over to the table where mi dad and Gavin were sitting.
"I got it dad." I said as I put the beer on the table and the trumpet under mi chair.
"Ya remember my lad Gavin? Ya met him when he

26

first came back from Australia."

"Aye, how ya going Dick Lad? Ya dad tells us ya gonna' play the trumpet for us tonight."

"Yeah, probably a couple of numbers Gavin."

"That'll make a change. We've had some right bloody awful acts on these past few weeks. Half of 'em couldn't sing for their bloody supper!" Eddie George was busy setting up his gear. I walked over the to the stage to say hello.

"G'day Eddie. How are ya mate?"

"Oh, hello lad. Ya made it then. I was hoping ya would. Did ya bring ya trumpet with ya then?"

"Yeah, it's at the table over there. Mi dad's keeping an eye on it for me."

"Well that's right good. I'll do a couple of spots on mi own for a start and then I'll call ya up on stage and introduce you as a guest artist. That sound alright to you then?"

"Yeah. no worries Eddie."

"I'll come and have a natter to yah before ya go on. That way, we can pick a few songs out that we both know. All right then?"

"Sounds alright to me Eddie. Thanks."

"No need to thank me lad as long as ya play well. We'll have a bit a fun. I get tired of playing on mi own sometimes, ya know." It was now around 8 o'clock. Eddie was due to start the nights entertainment. The MC walked out onto the small stage and announced the evenings show. Eddie launched into his first song. I asked mi dad how he liked the music, once Eddie had finished his first spot. True to form, both mi dad and Gavin made the same comment.

"I suppose he's all right." said Gavin. "What do they

27

call that kind of music anyway?"

"Probably middle of the road Gavin."

"Sounds to me like it's the end of the bloody road." said mi dad, who liked the old 1920's music. At about 9, Eddie called me over to the stage. We decided I would play 3 songs with him. Once we had worked out what key signatures we would use, Eddie announced me and I did my guest spot. After my 3 numbers were done, the crowd clapped like crazy. Eddie was over the moon with my performance.

"I didn't doubt you'd be able to play Richard." said Eddie. "But I had no idea at all that you'd be that good!"

"Well thanks Eddie. You're pretty good ya self mate."

"Oh, I'm not bad Richard but I'm nowhere in your league. You know your way around that trumpet, that's for sure. Come and have a natter with me at the end of the night when I'm packing up. If ya interested, ya can come out on a few jobs with me and I'll pay ya. I think we'd make a right good duo act, you and me."

That was the start of my part-time music career in the pubs and clubs of Yorkshire.

7

MEETING MI DANISH DREAM GIRL

It was now the end of November and Xmas was fast approaching. The weather had turned quite cold. It looked like snow was on the horizon. My life was now a far cry from my years spent in the Outback, working in 105 degree weather. When I was not going out for a few beers with a new or old friend, my time was spent sitting at home in front of the fire, in an effort to stay warm. Sitting at home on one's own with no distractions was a sure-fire way of tuning into my inner feelings and emotions. It was not because I was super interested in this type of inner work, it was more on the level of desperate need.

My biggest fantasy, in those days, was if I had a woman in my life, I would be happy. What a crock of shit this delusion turned out to be. Unbeknownst to me, I was soon to find out.

One evening, during the week, I had been sitting on my own for a while when the desire for female company came up so strong that it caused me to say out loud, "Fuck this for a joke. Fucked-up emotions or not, I'm off, out for a beer!" As I was getting dressed in some half-decent clothes, I remembered some bloke at the Foundry telling me about a little pub at a small village called Triangle. What made this pub more interesting than any other pubs was the fact the directly across the street and down a narrow lane was a woolen mill. In those days there were many mills in what is known as the Calder

Valley. Why was this mill different from any other mill? GIRLS! This particular mill had its own Hostel which was exclusively for girls to lodge at, full time. The local girls who lived in the surrounding area would go home every evening after work but the girls who'd come from places like Manchester, Oldham and Littleborough would stay at the Hostel. In fact, that is what they were called Hostel Girls. It was not uncommon, in a pub at Rippendon or Sowerby Bridge to here a couple of young blokes say, "Fuck this boring place. Let's catch a bus to Triangle and see if we can pick up a couple of Hostel Girls at the pub." Here I was thinking the same thought as I walked down Sowerby New Road to where I would catch the bus to Triangle.

"What can I get ya?" said the Publican as I entered the lounge bar.
"G'day mate, give us a pint please."
"Ya not from around these parts are ya?" he said as he pulled a pint of his best beer.
"I used to be years ago. I went to school here but when I left, I moved to Australia."
"I knew it. I couldn't quite pick the accent. I thought it might have been London or somewhere down South. So, which part of Australia d'ya come from?"
"Lake Cargelligo, New South Wales."
"Never heard of it. Is it near Sydney?"
"No mate. It's West of Sydney, hundreds of miles out in the Bush."
"I suppose it's pretty warm out there eh?"
"Yeah mate, she's a bit warmer than this place."
"Ya live around these parts?"

"Yeah, Up Sowerby New Road."

"Oh, I know where that is. So, ya visiting are ya?"

"Yeah, sort of. I've still got some relations who live there."

"Ya know, me and the missus were planning to go out to Australia in the late 50's but we bought into this pub instead and we've been here ever since. I still think about what our lives would have been like if we had taken the plunge."

"Ya could still go for a holiday, if ya wanted to."

"I suppose we could but the missus is not in real good health at the moment, so we'll have to wait and see."

"Well, I wish ya luck with that mate."

"Thanks, that's very kind of ya."

"A friend of mind told me there are quite a few girls who come in here, is that right?"

"Oh, aye lad, there's a Hostel across the road where they live. They mostly come in around this time a' night, if they're coming."

"Thanks for the chat mate. I guess I'll hang around for a while."

"Alright then. I'm off to clean up the other bar. Give us a shout when ya ready for another one."

I'd only been in the lounge bar for a half an hour when a small group of young girls walked in, laughing about some private joke they shared between themselves. Once they had ordered their drinks, they split up into two groups and settled into the comfortable lounge chairs. Two girls, in particular, that I noticed, sat on the opposite side of the room from the other girls and talked to each other in hushed voices. One of the girls was short and quite fat. She had straight brown, greasy-

31

looking hair. I noticed she had a fair few zits on her face. All in all, she was what's known in the Bush as a 'bush pig'. Her friend was the total opposite. She was about 5'8" tall with a slender body, blue eyes and blonde hair, and a lovely complexion. She was much more pleasing to the eye. 'That one will do me for the night', I thought as I watched them out of the corner of my eye. 'It's no good sitting here looking at them! Go over and offer to buy them a drink and see what happens.' I said to myself.

"How are ya girls?" I said to them as I casually walked over to their table. "Can I buy you a drink?"

"Yeah sure." said the chubby one. "We'll have half a beer each." 'Half a beer isn't gonna' cost much' I thought as I waited for the Publican to fill up the glasses. 'If nothing comes of it, well no great loss.'

Back at the table, I put the beers down and said "There ya go, half a pint each. D'ya mind it I sit down?"

"Yeah sure, sit down." said the bush pig.

"So, where are you from?" I asked. "I notice a foreign accent."

"We're from Aarhus in Denmark." said the chubby one.

"What are you doing in this place?" I asked.

"We're on a working holiday."

"How come ya ended up in Triangle?"

"A man, Billy Potter, got us a both a job working at the woolen mill."

"Oh, I know Billy Potter. I went to school with his younger brother. Where did ya meet him?"

"In Aarhus, at a bar. He offered to get us cheap tickets over here on the Merchant ship he was working on."

"Well, that's lucky eh?"

"What's ya names?"

"My name is Mina and my friend's name's Jonna."

"It's great to meet ya both. My name's Richard. I notice your friend Jonna doesn't say too much."

"That's because she can't speak very much English."

"That must be very difficult for her, especially working at the mill."

"Yeah, it is. I do all the translating for her but she gets very frustrated at times." Each time I asked Mina a question, Jonna would ask Mina to translate, so she could understand. At the end of the translation, she would flash me a great smile. After one translation, they both started to laugh.

"What's funny?" I said. Before Mina could answer, Jonna said something in Danish and Mina laughed.

"She just asked me not to translate."

"Why not?"

"Because she said she likes you. She said that you're a fine-looking man."

"Can you tell her thank you. I like the look of her. She's very pretty." Mina translated my words and they both started laughing again.

"Can you speak any English at all Jonna?"

"No speak English, very little."

"She's very shy about speaking English, Richard. She thinks people will laugh at her."

"Who cares? People around here can't speak any Danish, so what have they got to laugh about?" I said. Mina translated more and they both laughed. Our back and forth conversations continued on in this way until 10 O'clock, when the landlord called 'Last Orders'.

"Can I get you both a last drink?"

"No thanks," said Mina. "We've got to be back at the Hostel before 10:30 or we'll get locked out."

"Alright, no worries. Why don't I walk you both back down the lane? I wouldn't want you to get lost." I said jokingly. Mina laughed and said "I don't think that will happen but you can do, if you like." Once we arrived at the Hostel gate, I thanked Mina for translating and then said "Would you mind asking Jonna if I could take her out for a drink on Friday night?"

"Sure, I can do that." After a minute or so of translating, Mina said, "She'd like that very much but it will have to be at Triangle pub. She'd like me to be there to translate, so she can get to know you."

"Tell her, no worries. I understand. Ask her if 7's alright?"

"No problem." said Mina. "We'll meet you inside at 7." By this time, I had missed mi last bus. That was the last thing on my mind as I trudged along in the cold night. When I got back to my little, old miners' cottage it was quite late and really cold. There was no heating in the upstairs bedroom so I decided to sit in front of the gas fire for a while. It was not a hard decision to make. Sitting in mi chair with a smoke in mi hand and mi legs outstretched, warming mi feet in front of the fire, I thought about the night at the bar and the possibility of it turning into something good. 'Maybe my luck with women is starting to improve. She actually said she likes me. Now, all I have to do is get her away from Mina for a while and see where this budding new relationship will lead, if anywhere.' I thought.

I was not bothered by the fact that Jonna couldn't speak much English. The language of love and, hopefully, sex was a Universal language.

Over the next couple of days, my mind was running rampant, creating all sorts of fantasies. At the top of the list of fantasies was getting her to come back to my place and stay for the night. 'It's a good job I've got mi own cottage.' I thought. 'I can only imagine what it would be like asking mi mother if I could bring mi new girlfriend home to her place for the night!' Not only would her answer be a definite 'NO', I would never hear the last of it. Mi dad's house would've been out of the question even though he had three spare bedrooms. He would never let another woman over the threshold. Even the fat, old social worker wasn't allowed in his house to see how he was coping in his older years. The pavement was the closest she ever got to, before he told her to 'bugger off' and 'mind her own business.' By this time, mi feet were almost on fire and the rest of mi body was warm enough. Off with the gas fire and up the stone steps to mi cold bedroom I went. The bedroom seemed colder than normal tonight. Not surprisingly, there was ice on the inside of the window. I set the alarm clock for 5 o'clock, pulled back the blankets and dived into mi bed, with all mi clothes on. Once the blankets were pulled up over mi head, my mind went back to creating drama and fantasy about mi new Danish pastry. It didn't take long for Friday night to roll around. As I walked into the Triangle pub, in mi best going-out gear, I felt really happy. Would tonight end up like most other nights or would tonight be one to remember?

The Lounge bar was half-full. It didn't take long for me to spot Mina and Jonna sitting pretty much in the same place.

"G'day ladies." I said as I stood in front of their table, smiling from ear to ear. "Can I buy you both a drink?"

"Yeah sure." said Jonna. "Two half-pints." said Mina with a big grin on her face. Once I had the drinks, I carefully placed them on the table and sat miself down. After I lit up a smoke, I said to Jonna, "So, you've been kidding me. You really can speak English."

In Danish, she said to Mina, "What did he say?" After Mina translated, Jonna gave me a shy smile and said "A little."

The ice was now starting to crack a bit and the evening promised to be quite fruitful. Towards the end of the evening, a middle-aged bloke walked over to our table and said to Mina, "Ya ready to go? Sorry, I'm a bit late."

"Oh, that doesn't matter. I've been having a good time." Mina gathered up her purse, lighter and smokes off the table and said something in Danish to Jonna, who smiled at her and answered her in Danish.

"Richard." said Mina, "This is my friend Robert. He's taking me to an all-night party at his sisters place so you and Jonna will have to manage without my translating for the rest of the evening."

"What a shame." I said, not really meaning it. "I'm glad you've got someone to go to a party with."

"Robert's my boyfriend. We've known each other since we arrived here."

"How sweet. Well, have a great time Mina and you

too Robert."

"Before I forget Richard, Jonna can speak a little bit more English than she lets on. What she can't understand, try sign language. I'm sure you both will manage just fine without me." With that said, Mina and her boyfriend took off arm in arm. That left Jonna and me sitting at the table alone.

"Can I get you another drink Jonna?" I asked.

"Vacero." she said. I couldn't understand a word of Danish so I motioned to her empty glass and said, very slowly "Drink?"

"Ah! Yo mange tak." she said and gave me a smile. Standing at the bar, waiting for our drinks, I was remembering something I had heard in my travels that Swedish and Danish girls were pretty liberal when it came to sex. I was trusting that this little piece of information would turn out to be true. So far, I hadn't had much luck with English girls. It seemed that the ones I had met wanted some kind of commitment before they would hop in the sack for a root! In England, they call it a 'shag'.

For two people who couldn't understand each other's language, my first time alone with Jonna didn't go too bad considering I was speaking broken pigeon English, using sign language and drawing pictures on the back of beer mats. The landlord called 'last orders' and soon I was walking Jonna back down the lane to the Hostel. A couple of young girls walked past as we stood outside the Hostel gate.

"How long before the Hostel closes?" I asked one of the girls.

"It doesn't close for another hour. It's Friday night."

"Ya mean it stays open an hour longer on Fridays?"
"Yeah, Friday and Saturdays 'cause there's no work on Sundays."
"Thanks for the information ladies." I said as they giggled and disappeared through the gate.
Somehow, I made Jonna understand the later curfew time. I convinced her to show me around the mill which was a good thing as the weather that night was really cold. As Jonna showed me where she worked, I was more interested in finding a warm, cosy place where we could make out. Once we got to the wool-sorting room, it was like a dream come true. There were numerous bales of wool that were broken open and the fleeces were scattered all over the floor. The smell of the place and the wool bales everywhere immediately took me back to the shearing sheds in the bush.

After a bit of coaxing on my part, I convinced Jonna to sit on a pile of fleeces that I had thrown together as a makeshift bed. There wasn't a lot time left by now and the Hostel gate would soon be closing. I had to make my intentions know to her in as clear a way as possible through actions, as words were far too limiting, at this stage. Half an hour later found Jonna and miself putting our clothing back together and pulling lumps of wool out of her hair before returning her to the Hostel. We had one last kiss and cuddle before a fat old woman came to the gate and said, "In or out, which is it gonna' be. It's just past curfew time." One last kiss and Jonna walked through the gate into the Hostel. The old woman gave me a dirty look as she secured the chain and lock around the iron gate.

Back in mi cottage, after walking home again, the gas fire was going full bore and steam was rising off mi socks as I sat in mi favorite chair smoking an Old Holburn hand-rolled cigarette. 'She seems to like me a lot.' I thought. Even though we didn't know each other very well, this relationship might turn into a regular girlfriend situation, or she might not want to see me again.' Back and forth, the mind went trying its best to assess what had transpired a few hours previously. Not being able to come to come to a decision, I said, 'fuck it', turned the fire off and headed for bed.

8

THE BIGGEST SHOCK

It was now almost Xmas. As it turned out, the local people were spot on with their weather forecasting and a thick blanket of fresh, white snow covered the roof tops and trees. My relationship with Jonna was still going strong. She had even agreed to stay overnight at my place a couple of times. Mina had been a great help in our relationship as she had been teaching Jonna lots of everyday English. I, of course, was learning a few simple Danish words which also helped the situation along.

One evening, as the three of us sat in the lounge bar, a whole different ball-game came into play. Mina made a big announcement that she had a ticket booked on the Ferry from Harritch to Esberg and she would be returning to Denmark for Xmas. When I asked her for how long, she replied, "For good. I'm not coming back."
"What about Jonna? Will she be going with you?"
"No. I don't think so."
 After a few seconds of silence, Mina said, "Jonna has something to tell you."
After talking to each other for a while, in Danish, Mina blurted out the life-changing news to me.
"Jonna is pregnant! She's missed two periods."
I did my best to hide the shock on my face. My hand dived for the glass of beer and I took a big gulp. My other hand picked up the smokes and lit one up in a faster than normal fashion. When I finally looked at Jonna, her face was a blank stare. She quickly

looked down at the table for her smokes and lit one up, almost as fast as I had. Mina was the first to break the silence. "A bit of a shock for you Richard?"

"A bit! That's an understatement Mina."

"Listen Richard, you and I need to have a talk. I'm going to tell Jonna to go home now. I don't want her asking me what we're talking about every two minutes."

Mina explained the situation to Jonna. Jonna, reluctantly, agreed to go home early and that I would come down to the Hostel later on so she and I could sort things out. After I filled up our glasses, Mina explained to me everything she knew about Jonna for the past three years of knowing her. "First of all, Richard, you do know she's only 18, right?"

"She's 19 pretty soon eh?"

"That's right, but although Jonna may look grown up because of her figure, I can tell you now, from my own experience that for her age, she's very immature. Since I've been friends with her, we have had many arguments and differences of opinions. If you want to be with her or marry her, you should know that her mind is quite unstable. She will, all of a sudden, flare up over nothing. I know her whole family and except for one of her brothers, I feel that there's something not quite right with any of them."

"Can you give me any examples?"

"Well, her youngest sister, who's about 8 goes to a Special Education school for retarded children. One of her other brothers is a kleptomaniac who has been in and out of Juvenile Detention schools. Her father is a porn addict and one of her other sisters prostitutes herself for whatever she needs. Do I need to carry on?"

"Oh shit! I had no idea."

"How could you? You barely know each other. The fact that her English is so bad doesn't help either."

"If I didn't, at least, look after her or marry her, what's the alternative? There's no such thing as abortion in this country that I'm aware of." I said.

"No that seems to be so, but Denmark is a completely different place. Abortions are quite easy to get there. I had one myself once."

Once Mina had given me all the background, she could on Jonna, she said, "This is my suggestion Richard. I'm going to go back to the Hostel now and tell Jonna what we talked about, alright?"

"Yeah, but won't she be angry you telling all her family secrets?"

"For sure. She'll be pissed off but this is how I see it Richard. In the short time I've known you, I can tell that you're a good man. It doesn't seem fair to me that you have to make a big decision like this, with no information about the situation you're in. I've already told Jonna that she was stupid for having sex when she'd missed taking some of the pills."

"Was she pissed?"

"Oh yeah. I told her the truth, so who cares."

"Do you think she missed taking some of the pills on purpose?" I asked.

"No, she wouldn't do that."

"How do you know?"

"Because she doesn't want to be pregnant. She's freaking out now."

"Do you think she loves me?"

"No, how can she? You haven't known each other

42

long enough. She did say she likes you very much, and for Jonna, that's as good as it gets for now. Richard, I think it would be a wise thing for you to go straight home tonight so I can have a long talk with her and make sure she fully understands the position she's in. I'll tell her you're coming to the pub tomorrow night. I can translate for you both."
"Sounds good to me Mina. I really appreciate your helping out in this situation."
"That's alright. I don't want to see either of you forced into something that you don't want to be in."
"Let me ask you this. If I didn't want to go through with this pregnancy, what would happen to her?"
"In that case, I'd buy her a ticket when we got to the Ferry and she would pay me back when we got home."
"And the abortion?"
"Abortions are free in Denmark and as her friend, I'd go with her as moral support." Mina finished her beer and said, "We'll meet you here tomorrow night alright?"
"Alright." I said and shook her hand, before she took off back to the Hostel to make Jonna aware of all that we had discussed.

The following evening, Jonna and Mina were already in the Lounge bar waiting for me. I gave them a wave and ordered myself a beer.
"How are you?" said Mina as I put mi beer on a spare coaster.
"I'm fine Mina. Hey Jonna, how are ya?" I said as I leaned across the table to give her a reassuring kiss on the cheek.
"I ok Richard."

"Ok Richard." said Mina. "This is how it is. I spoke to Jonna at length about your situation last night and we came up with a couple of options. She knows I'll buy her a ticket back to Denmark so she can get an abortion. If you care enough about her, she could stay here with you and you can both try to make a go of it. Another option could be that Jonna wants you to come and live in Denmark, with her. So, what do you think?"

"First off, there's no way I can live in Denmark now as I have my cottage to pay off." Mina translated to Jonna what I said. A look of disappointment spread across her face.

"You could rent it out." said Jonna in Danish.

Once Mina translated, I said "That's not possible. If I rent it out and they don't pay, after a while, I'll end up losing it. Mina, please make it clear to Jonna that there are only two viable options for me. If she stays in England, she can live with me and I'll take care of her. I'll even marry her if that's what she wants. The only other option for me is for her to go back to Denmark to live and get an abortion." Mina translated my feelings to Jonna, who didn't look at all happy.

After some conversations together, Mina said in a frustrated voice, "I told you Richard, Jonna is not very mature. She says she doesn't want to be pregnant and she doesn't want a baby. I told her that she should've thought about that before, not after. Now she's really pissed with me. By the way Richard, I'm leaving here by taxi really early in the morning or I won't be able to connect with the Ferry, so this is what I suggest. Jonna is not going to make

44

a decision either way, if she thinks she can get you to agree to living in Denmark."

"That's not gonna' happen Mina. I explained why."

"I know. The only answer I can see is for you to tell her, in English, that you're going home now and you'll come back here tomorrow night. If she's here, she's staying. If she's not, you'll know she's gone with me. Now, give her a hug and walk out."

"Mina, again, I want to thank you for everything you've done."

"That's not a problem Richard. I know you'd help me out if I needed it. Now, give me a hug and say farewell."

After I'd hugged Mina and said farewell, I stood in front of Jonna and said, "If ya here tomorrow night or not, either way I'll have an answer."

Jonna stood up and I gave her the best long hug and kiss I could.

As I let her go, she started to cry. I walked away, keeping my emotions hidden.

The Sowerby bus stopped right outside where I lived but instead of going straight home, I walked across the street to the small Off-license store and bought some tobacco and a couple of Newcastle Browns.

Back home, I lit the fire, pulled mi armchair up in front of it, kicked off mi shoes, rolled a smoke and opened a bottle. 'What a fucking mess I've created.', I thought. 'Instead of it being a lot of fun as I imagined it would be, it's a fucking disaster. All of these problems I created and what for? A couple of fucks!'

"Right!" said an inner voice.

45

"Why didn't ya tell me that before?" I said inwardly.
"Would you have listened?"
"Fuck you!" I said.

I can't let her manipulate me into living in Denmark
at her parents' house. What if we have a big
argument and her parents kick me out? Where the
fuck would I go then? Where would I work over
there? I have no education or skills other than
shearing and I can't speak the language. I'm in a
'wait and see' situation till tomorrow night when my
fate will be decided! Then, another horrible thought
came up. What's mi mother gonna' say when she
finds out. I can already hear her now. "You got that
girl pregnant on purpose just to show me up in front
of mi friends and neighbors!" Mi mother lived with
mi dad for 12 years without getting married and to
boot, she had 3 kids with him before she left him.
I'm showing her up? Oh well, I'll just remind her of
the bastard standing in front of her that she gave
birth to.

The best thing for me will be if Jonna decides to go
back to Denmark with Mina. If she decides to have
an abortion, well that's her decision. If she decides
to have the baby then I will take on the
responsibility of paying money for its upkeep. I've
got Mina's address and phone number and she's got
my address. If Jonna decides to go that route, I'll
know soon enough. As a boy, growing up, my
mother would always say "You made ya bed lad,
now you'll have to lay in it!" Every time mi dad
heard her say it, he would always say to me, "Don't
bloody well believe that old tripe boy. If you find a

better bed, jump in that one!" If I had my druthers, I'll jump into another bed, seeing as I'm only a young man but I have no options in this drama. I'll have to wait and see what life has in store for me.

9

WHAT HAVE YA DONE NOW, YORKY?

The night of nights had finally arrived. As I stood outside the Triangle Pub door, I thought, 'Will this be the night that changes my life or not?' Taking a deep breath, I pushed open the door and headed for the Lounge bar. The place was almost empty except for a few locals sitting at the bar. Jonna sat at her usual table, minus Mina. I gave her a wave and a smile, ordered a pint and walked over to where she sat.

"G'day sweetie. How are ya?"

"I ok Richard."

"Has Mina gone back to Denmark?"

"Mina go. I no go back Hostel. No good."

"No worries." I said.

"I live your house."

"No problem. Your English sounds better."

"I no like speak English. Me no good speak!"

"That's not true Jonna. You speak good English. I understand you very well."

"No, me no good!" Jonna said as she lit up a smoke. She just sat there saying nothing. It was obviously up to me to make conversation if we were to talk to each other.

"Where are your clothes?" I said as I motioned to my shirt and jacket.

"Clothes at Hostel. Me pick up."

"Alright, no worries Jonna. We'll go to the Hostel as soon as we finish our beers." She gave me a little smile. I could only presume she understood me.

When we picked up Jonna's luggage, which was not very much, we caught a double-decker bus back to Sowerby Bridge and a connecting bus up Sowerby New Road to my cottage. Once inside, I turned on the fire to heat up the room as it was quite cold due to the icy weather and snow. When she was warm enough, I said, "Let's take your bags upstairs. I've got a cupboard for you and you can have half of the wardrobe." When her clothes were in the drawers and the few items she had were hung up on her side of the wardrobe, I made her a cup of tea. I showed her where everything could be found. Sitting in front of the gas fire on the couch I had just moved, we sat there looking at the fire not saying much at all.

Eventually Jonna said, "This house old."
"Yeah, it's an old cottage Jonna but it's a good one."
"No good house, no toilet."
"Yeah, there's a toilet Jonna. It's outside remember? You used it last time you stayed overnight."
"Toilet no good!"
'Oh fuck', I thought to myself. 'She's only been living here for an hour and already she's fucking complaining. I hope this isn't going to become a yardstick for the future?'
Eventually she said, "Mothers house good house."
"I'm sure it is but this is a good house as well. It's warm and dry and plenty big enough for you and me."
"I no like!" I was doing my best to have as much patience with her as I could, seeing as it was me who got her pregnant. She was now living with me in a strange country.
"You'll get used to it, don't worry, just relax and

49

enjoy yourself."
"Where is Television?"
"I don't have one. I don't like them."
"I like."
"Well, maybe I'll get you one at some stage."
"No stereo?"
"No stereo Jonna."
"Denmark everybody have big stereo!"
"I'm happy for them but we don't have one."
"How do you like the new gas fire?"
"Fire OK. Kitchen no good."

 I decided not to comment this time as I thought to miself, 'I'll let her get it all out of her system. At the rate she's going there's not much left to like so that will be the end of it', or so I thought.

Little did I know that this was only the beginning of the nightmare that I had created for myself. It was getting quite late now. I asked Jonna, "What time do you start work at the mill in the morning."
"What work? What time start? 8, but I no like this work. Too hard."
"Maybe we can find you a better job and later in your pregnancy you'll probably be able to stop working."
"I stop work!" she said with a smile on her face.
"No, not now. We will have to save money for the baby." The smile disappeared as fast as it appeared and she said, "I no like baby. I no like work."
"Jonna, why didn't you go back to Denmark with Mina instead of staying here? You don't seem to like anything about this place."
"England good place for party."

"Oh, I see. Well I don't think we'll be doing much partying but that doesn't mean we can't go out to the pub on a weekend."

"I no like pub. I like disco and dancing."

"Let's see what happens eh."

Neither of us spoke for quite a while as we sat on the couch, warming up our feet. After a while I said "Jonna, it's getting late. We better go to bed. I'm on early shift at the Foundry. I've got to get up at 5."

She was in no hurry to move away from the fire. I thought to myself, 'Fuck this for a joke!' as I bent over and turned off the fire.

"Let's go love."

"I go toilet."

"You just want a pee?"

"Yes, I piss."

"You know it's really cold out there so if you like we can use a bucket during the night and empty it in the morning. That's what we all did when we lived on the Moors, in our farmhouse."

"I no like piss-bucket. I go outside."

"Suit yourself but I'm telling ya, if you need to go at 3 in the morning, you won't like going outside and the seat will be bloody freezing." Once she was back inside, I locked the door and said "Hurry up, let's get into bed. It's getting cold down here."

By the time I was in bed, Jonna was still sitting on the side of the double bed. I said to her "Come on, hurry up and get your nightgown on and get into bed. It's a cold bloody night!" Reluctantly, she started to get undressed and once she was down to her bra and knickers she said, "Sluck din lous!"

"I can't understand. What d'ya mean?"

"Lous!" she said and pointed to the light.

"Oh, light. You mean turn off the light. Why? I'm enjoying watching you."

"I no like you see." Once the light was out all I saw was a dark shadow pulling on a nightgown and getting into bed. When she was in bed with the blankets pulled right up under her chin, I scooted up close to her and put my arm under the back of her neck. Then I put my right arm over her belly and pulled her closer. After we had a few kisses, I let my right hand start to wander down. As soon as it reached her pussy she grabbed my hand and said "I no like! I have hoypin."

"What's hoypin?"

It didn't take a rocket scientist to figure out that she had a headache. Sex would not be on the menu tonight! Headache or not, that didn't stop me trying a couple more times. It didn't stop her saying 'hoypin' a few more times.

From that point, we didn't speak for the rest of the night. I just lay there watching what was going on with my feelings and listening to my mind as it created all sorts of dramas. 'Fuck me dead', I thought. Apart from a couple of times when we slept on the couch in front of the fire all night, this is the first night that she's been officially living here as my wife and what happens? A big fat nothing! It's almost like a honeymoon night, without the sex.'

I was not very fucking happy with this turn of events. Here I am, 22 years old, laid in bed with an 18 year old girl who I have got pregnant and no pussy on the first night! I hope this is not a sign of things to come! If so, then I've fucked up worse than

52

I can ever imagine. My mind wandered back to the last time we had sex, on the couch, in front of the fire. I know I'm no Romeo or a high-priced Gigolo but I feel I am aware and attentive to a woman's needs in this type of situation. No matter what I did, she didn't seem to move around much. At one point, I thought 'I could light up a smoke and then stub it out on her arse. That would get her moving!' I even asked her if she liked it and although she said "yes", she wasn't, what I would say, over the moon with joy! I even thought I should have just sent her back to Denmark with Mina. I dismissed the should and shouldn't idea as that was proof-positive, it was too late in the game for that. All these post-mortem thoughts about our first real night together were not helping at all so I reverted to my old standard line, which was FUCK IT! and went to sleep.

The following morning the alarm clock started ringing like crazy at 5 o'clock. Throwing the blankets back and sitting on the side of the bed for a minute, I watched Jonna grab the blankets and pull them all over to her side. I had to be at work on the early morning shift at 6 so I had no spare time for an early morning shag, which didn't look as if it would have been too promising anyway.

Downstairs, I put the fire on to heat up the room which was really cold, first thing. After the tea was brewed, I sat on the couch and rolled a smoke as I sipped the hot tea. I would have to get Jonna up at 5:30 before I left for work. When she was living at the Hostel, she would only have 30 or 40 yards to walk to work but this morning she have to catch a

bus or walk down to Sowerby Bridge and catch a
bus to Triangle Mill.
"Come on Jonna. Get up! It's Monday. Work day!"
"Go away! I no like work."
"Come on, get up! You've got to go to work or you'll
lose your job. There's hot tea in the kitchen and you
can make some breakfast for yourself before you go.
I'm off to work now."

Very begrudgingly, she slowly pulled the blankets
back and swung her legs over the side of the bed.
"Is fucking cold this morning! Me no like cold!"
"Neither do I but there's not much we can do about
that. Put your dressing gown on. That will help. By
the way, don't forget to turn off the gas fire before
you go. I'm off now or I'll be late. See ya tonight
when ya get home."

With that said, I gave her a kiss and said "See ya.
Don't forget to lock the door when you leave."
As I walked out the bedroom, I heard her say
"Fucking work, me no like!"
Standing outside at the bus stop waiting for the
Double-Decker to come, I stamped my feet up and
down on the snowy pavement. I thought about my
life in the Outback. 'It's probably 100 degrees in
Lake Cargelligo today and here I am standing at a
fuckin' bus stop, freezing cold.' The bus arrived a bit
late this morning due to the weather. Once I got off
at my stop, I'd have to run down the valley road to
the Foundry so I wasn't late or they'd dock off some
of my money. I finished work at 2. If I ran up the
valley road to the top of Sowerby, I'd be in time to
catch the pub before it closed for the afternoon at 3

o'clock.

'That's another stupid law they've got in England,' I thought. 'Who the fuck ever heard of pubs closing in the afternoon! Afternoon is the hottest part of the day, in the Bush. If they closed up then, they'd have a fucking riot on their hands.'

Once I got to the pub, I headed for the tap room where all the blokes did their drinking and ordered miself a pint of Best.

"Dick Lad!" said Jim, one of mi old school mates. "Where've ya been? I haven't seen ya for a while. How's that little Danish Pastry of yours?"

"Don't ask Jim." I said as I knocked back half of the pint in a couple of large gulps.

"Jesus mate, by the way you're knocking back that pint, things can't be too good. Am I right?"

"Pretty much." I said as I swallowed the remainder of the beer.

"Give us ya glass, Dick. I'll buy ya a beer before closing."

Once we had our beers, we sat at one of the spare tables and had a good natter about the ups and downs of living with a woman.

"Well Dick Lad, I feel for ya mate. My problem is the opposite of yours. My missus can't get enough of it. She'd shag me every night if I didn't say no. I'm the one who has a sore back and a headache in my place when it's time to go to bed. I've already got 3 kids and another one on the way. I think I'm gonna' have to go to the doctors and see about gettin' cut, before I go broke!"

Before I left the pub, Jim said to me "By the way

Dick Lad, I'm off hunting rabbits next Sunday morning with the ferrets. I bought a new Lurcher last week and I'm dying to try her out. Ya wanna' come out with me?"

"That sounds like a plan Jim. I'll let ya know towards the end of the week. It depends how mi new girlfriends settling in, ya know what I mean?"

"Ya don't have to explain to me Dick. I'm a veteran!"

Back at mi cottage, I put the fire on and dried mi boots off from tramping around in the snow. I went into the kitchen to turn the electric jug on and make miself a cup of hot tea. "Fuck me dead!" I said as I looked around the kitchen. When I lived here on mi own, I cleaned up after miself and left everything tidy so I didn't come home to a messy place. Jonna's only been living here less than a day and the kitchen's a fucking mess. I'm gonna have to talk to her tonight and lay down a few 'ground rules' about living here. She said her mother's house was a great place but I don't see how it could be, if it was left like mi kitchen! She never even put the lid on the jam! It was left with the lid off with a knife sticking out of it. When I looked in the jar it had crumbs stuck around the top half of it. Now, I am by no means a 'neat-freak' but everywhere I lived in the Outback on mi own, I always lived clean and tidy. Well, it's no good leaving it like this. I'd better clean the place up so we can make something to eat for dinner tonight.

At around 6 o'clock, I was sitting on the couch having a smoke and a cuppa tea when the door opened and Jonna walked in.

"How are ya Jonna?" I asked.

"I no good. Is long way to go work!" She took off her coat and threw it over one of the chairs and was just about to walk over to the fire when I said, "Ya hang ya coat up behind the door and if ya boots are wet, take 'em off over there, then carry 'em over to the fire and we'll dry them." She didn't look too pleased about being told to hang her coat up and said, "Shoes no wet!"

"Alright, no worries. Come and get warm, you must be freezing!"

"Me no cold. Denmark cold."

"Come and sit down and I'll get you a hot cup of tea."

Once she was sat in front of the fire, drinking her tea and smoking a fag, I very tactfully told her what was expected of her so that we could live together, with a minimum of drama. After I finished, she said, "Me keep mother's house clean."

"Alright, so why not clean up after yourself here. Did you sleep in?"

"No, I up at 6 o'clock."

"So, why not clean up after yourself?"

"This old house. Not new like my mothers." This piece of information actually gave me the shits as I had spent a lot of time and money fixing up the cottage so it was clean and comfy. Maybe it would have been better to have a bit more patience but I took her comments about my cottage as an insult.

"Hey Jonna, if you think my place is an old dump and you don't want to keep it clean, you can always fuck off back to the Hostel." With that said, she lost

57

it!

"Fuck you Richard. I go Denmark! I no live here and no go Hostel." She burst into tears and took off up the stairs. 'Oh shit! Now what have I done? I had to say something. I'm not living in a pig sty. It's usually men that are messy slobs, not women.'
I heard mi dad's voice in mi head saying, 'I've been as happy as a pig in shit since I told that wench of a mother of yours to sling her bloody hook and don't forget to take ya bloody kids with ya'. I never wanted 'em in the first place!' What the fuck am I gonna' do now? It's obvious she thinks she's made a mistake staying here with me 'cause if she was happy she wouldn't be so angry. I suppose I'd better to upstairs and try to talk some sense into her, otherwise we aren't gonna' last long at this rate. I sat on the side of the bed for about half an hour, doing my best to explain to her that I wanted her in my life and I really cared about her. It was like talking to a brick wall! Every time I said something she didn't like she said, "Me no understand English." and pulled the covers over her head.

In the end, I'd had enough. I said, "You no understand English? Then fuck you! See if you understand that!" I got up off the bed and just as I walked out of the room she said,
"Fuck you bastard!"
'Jesus', I thought. 'I must be getting through to her. At least she's communicating now and it sounds like her vocabulary has expanded by a few more words!'
It was now 9 o'clock and I hadn't eaten anything since lunchtime. Jonna had been upstairs in bed for a couple of hours now so I decided to go upstairs and

58

see if she wanted anything to eat.

"Hey Jonna, ya wanna eat something?" At first, she didn't answer but after a I shook her a few times she said, "Go away! I no like you!"

"Please ya self then." and I took off back downstairs.

Directly across the street from mi cottage was a fairly big corner store. There was also a Grog shop that sold all kinds of alcohol. Last but not least was a blessing from the Gods. A fair dinkum, old-fashioned fish and chip shop that sold the real thing, Icelandic cod and freshly fried chips. None of the modern, pre-cooked stuff. The best part of it was the cost, 2 shillings and sixpence, which would be roughly 50 cents in today's money.

"Fish and chips love." I said to the woman behind the counter. "Can you put a scoop of batter bits on it while you're at it?"

"How are ya lovey." she said, flashing me a big smile. "How ya settling in across the road there?"

"Pretty good. It was a bit of a mess when I bought it but I've fixed it up and it's really quite comfortable."

"Mrs. Higgins lives in Number 6. She's your next-door neighbor, right?"

"Yeah, she is."

"She comes in here all the time. I've known her for years. I knew her before she got married. I've been in her house ya know, they're right grand little cottages. She did hers up when they first moved in. It's a bit of a shame they're gonna' pull 'em down in 5 years."

"Yeah, it is. Just as well I don't plan on living here that long."

"So ya going back to Australia then are ya?"

"I sure am."

"Don't ya like it here then?"

"No, not really. I grew up in the Outback and I miss it. How did ya know I'm from Australia?"

"Ya mother told me. She's been coming in here for years. She's a good woman is your mother, ya know. I had to stop miself asking her about you when ya first left home."

"Why?"

"Well every time I said, 'How's your Richard doing in Australia', she'd start crying. Anyway love, ya fish and chips are ready. Ya wanted bits on 'em right?"

"Yeah that would be great."

"I'll let you put your own salt and vinegar on, then I'll wrap 'em up for ya. That'll be half a crown love." I gave her the money and as I walked out she said, "Say hello to ya mother for me."

"No worries." I said and went next door to the Off License Grog Shop. I bought 2 bottles of Newcastle Brown in case Jonna had changed her mind and decided to get up out of bed. The snow had started to come down quite heavy now as I crossed the main road and walked up the passage way back home. I couldn't wait to get back inside mi warm cottage and eat mi fish and chips in front of a warm fire. Once I'd finished eating, I washed it down with a room-temperature beer and rolled miself a fat 'roll ya own' smoke.

The second bottle of beer looked quite lonely sitting on the carpet at the side of the couch so I opened it up with mi tobacco tin, a trick I'd learned in the

Bush. The metal cap made a popping sound as it shot off the bottle and hit the ceiling. 'Fucking lovely.' I thought as I drank it straight out the bottle. 'Outback champagne and English fish and chips! What more could a man ask for?' The only thing missing now was a good shag, which was out of the question tonight!
The next couple of days passed without any trauma. Jonna seemed to be slowly adjusting to her new life. All seemed well 'til the shit hit the fan on Thursday. My usual habit was to have a couple of beers with a few of my mates before heading home at 3 o'clock.

It had been snowing on the tops of the walls and the surrounding fields. Apart from it being so bloody cold, I loved the winter as everything looked like a picture postcard. The rooks and crows that perched on the highest dead branches of the trees, squawked out a raucous tune as if to say, "It's bloody cold!"

I was so happy today. I saw myself pick up handfuls of snow and squeeze them into tight balls and then launch them at a distant road sign to test out my aim. Walking up the narrow passage to my cottage, I hummed a Xmas carol.

~10~

IT'S NOW WAR!

Outside my one and only door was an old-fashioned boot scraper set into one of the flag stones. Seeing as it was there, I made good use of it and scraped as much snow off mi boots as possible, rather than walk it inside and have it melt all over the new carpet I had installed.

The key to the door was about 4 inches long and was made out of, what looked like, old iron. I shoved it in the lock and tried to turn it as I had done many times before. Today, for some reason, it wouldn't turn. I tried turning it in the opposite way which would have locked it. The lock made a 'clunking' sound as the neck passed the point of no return. 'Fuck me dead!' I thought 'Jonna has gone off to work this morning and forgotten to lock the door. Oh well, too late now. I'll have to explain to her how important it is to lock the door when she leaves. Otherwise, one day we'll be coming home to an empty house.' The lock chinked again with a turn of the key and I pushed the door open. WHOOSH! A blast of warm air hit me in the face at lightning speed I thought 'She forgot to turn the gas fire off when she left for work!'

Walking over the threshold, I got the shock of mi life. There was Jonna, curled up asleep on the couch in front of the gas fire that was cranking out the heat full blast! Taking mi boots off and hanging mi coat up behind the door, I walked over to the couch and gave Jonna a couple of shakes. It took a couple of shakes before she woke up. Once she was back in the land of the living I said, with quite a bit of concern, "What's the matter love? Aren't ya feeling well? Are ya sick?"

"Me no sick."

"What are ya doing home at this time? You don't normally get home till six."

"Me no work!" she said as she reached for a fag and lit it up.

"What d'ya mean? Did you have morning sickness or a headache?" I asked her about a headache as she took an unusual amount of headache pills. The brand she preferred, Head-X, was the strongest type one could get, over the counter.

"So, if you're not sick and don't have a headache then what are you doing home?"

"I no work!"

"Did you get fired?"

"No, I tell you, I no work."

"You mean you had a day off?"

"No! You not understand English! I no work!"

"Ya mean ya quit?"

"Yes, me no work no more."

My jolly mood that I was experiencing walking home had just flown out the window with this new piece of information she had just delivered. If I was understanding her correctly, what she was saying was, "I'm sick of working so I'm going to stay home all day." I could feel the temperature of my blood starting to rise. I went into the kitchen and put the electric jug on for a cup of tea. As soon as the tea was brewed, I made 2 cups and then took them into the living room and sat down on the couch, next to her.

"Alright Jonna, we need to have a talk about this not working, situation."

"Me no work anymore."

"Don't you like the job, is that it?"

"Me don't like work."

"Well, if you don't like the job at the mill, ya might be able to find another job that you do like but it's going to be difficult because of your lack of English."

"Me not work anymore. Stay home!"

I did my very best to explain to her that she couldn't just quit working because she didn't feel like it. Apart from paying off the cottage, all of my other expenses were now doubled because she was living with me. It didn't make any difference. I tried a different approach, "Look Jonna, had we not met each other and you were still living at the Hostel with Mina, you would have had to keep working. If not, they would have made you leave and then what would you have done?" Still there was no change in her attitude. She was behaving like a spoilt child. The time had rolled along as it usually does. The wall clock now read 9 o'clock. I was fresh out of ideas and had run out of patience. I said, "Alright Jonna, this is how it is. I'm going to ask you one more time and that's it. Are you going to work tomorrow or not?"

"You fucking stupid man Richard. You Snak, Snak, Snak (talk, talk, talk) for work. I tell you, I NO FUCKING WORK!"

Now she was really angry! She started shouting at me in Danish, which I couldn't understand a bloody word of. Any resemblance of patience I had was now long gone, replaced by frustration and anger. I said, "You fucking Danish bitch, That's it! I've had a fucking gut-full of your childish fucking nonsense. Back to the fucking Hostel you go!"

"Fuck you Richard. I no go. I stay here."

"No fucking way Jonna. You haven't made any fucking effort at all to do a thing since you've been here. Ya won't even clean up after yourself. Ya don't wanna' work anymore and to boot, you've suddenly decided ya' don't want sex anymore! Well, ya know what! You're fucking outa' here! You're not making my life a fucking misery. I may not have been the happiest bloke on the planet before I met you but I certainly wasn't miserable!"

With that, I grabbed her by the arm and dragged her off the couch towards the door. As she kicked and screamed, I managed to open the door with one hand while still holding her with my other hand. I dragged her outside into the snow-ladened cobble stone road and I let go of her! She just sat there, in her nightdress, in the snow with venom and stubbornness in her eyes and told me to get fucked in Danish. That I could understand!

Back inside, with the door bolted up tight, I went upstairs to the bedroom and grabbed most of her clothes and jammed them into her bag. 'Fucking crazy bitch!', I thought as I zipped up her bag. Back downstairs, I snuck a look out of the curtained window, there she was, still where I left her, sat in the snow. Once the door was unbolted, I threw her

65

bag towards her.

"If ya gonna' start acting more mature instead of like a spoilt brat, ya can come back inside, till the morning." She lifted her head to look at me and said, "Fuck off cunt! Me no work!"

I was now frustrated about not being able to get through to her. I was angry about the situation I had created. I sat on the couch finishing off the now strong, cold tea and rolled myself a smoke.

'Jesus Christ almighty' I thought. 'What the fuck have I done?' An inner voice said to me, 'Now you've really done it sport! You've created the same type of relationship ya mother and father had all those years ago. All ya dreams and fantasies of a good, loving relationship with a woman have just blown up in your face. what are ya gonna do now?' The mind went silent for a few seconds and then said, 'Remember what Mina said about her family? Her brothers and sisters are crazy, thieves and whores. Why would you expect Jonna to be any different?'

'I thought I'd be able to help her and make her happy.' was my answer. 'How is that possible?' said the voice. 'Ya not happy ya self unless ya drinking beer and partying.'

'I'm not as crazy as that bitch is.'

'Maybe not, but you got her pregnant and now you're stuck with her!'

'No, I'm not. She won't last long out there in the snow. She'll put some clothes on and catch a bus back to the hostel.'

Half an hour had now gone by. I got up from the couch and peeped through the curtain to see if she'd gone. To my disappointment and amazement there she was, still sitting in the snow in her nightdress, staring down at her legs. 'Fucking shit, she hasn't even got the brains to put some clothes on or sit on her bag!'

Back on the couch I heard mi dad's voice in mi head, 'If brains were gunpowder, that lad of yours wouldn't have enough to blow his bloody hat off!' 'He's your son as well!' said mi mother's voice.

All sorts of negative voices were now battling with each other in mi mind to put their 2 pence in, which was really pissing me off. I have always been brutally honest with miself, even as a child. I had to admit to miself that some of the inner voices were scoring major points. I looked at the wall clock and it read 10 o'clock. I got up off the couch for another sneaky look out the window. 'She's bound to be gone now', I thought, as I pulled the curtain back slightly. "Fuck me Rome." I said out loud. "I don't believe it! She's still fucking sitting there. How could anybody be so fucking stubborn, not realizing, at the time, she was a reflection of myself! It was 11 at night. She was still sitting in the snow. In the end it was my compassion working overtime that overruled my anger. How could anyone sit out there in freezing cold weather, in just a night dress.? There is no way in hell that Jonna is of sound mind. In order to get rid of her or help her to realize that this type of behavior was not going to be tolerated, I opened the door and told her to come back inside.

Five minutes went by before she picked up her bag

and came inside. Sitting on the couch in front of the fire, she said nothing. Instead, she opened her handbag and took out a bottle of Head-X tablets, pulled out the cotton wool and dropped 2 into her hand. She swallowed them straight, without any water and then lit one of her cigarettes, all the while not saying a fucking word.

In as calm a voice as I could find, I said to her, "Jonna, this is the end of the line for you. There's no way I'm living like this. As soon as I've got enough money, you are going back to Denmark, like it or not."

"I no go back. I stay here."

"There's no fucking way you're staying with me. If you refuse to go back, I'm calling the Social services to see about having you committed!"

"Me no understand."

"Hospital for crazy people." I said.

"Me no go to crazy hospital."

"I don't know how it is in Denmark but in this country, crazy people who are in danger of hurting themselves get put in an institution for their own welfare." I don't know what part of my talking she understood. A look of fear now spread across her face. I was now quite worried that she would do herself some kind of injury when I went up to bed. I didn't have any options as it was now past midnight. I had to be up at 5 in the morning for work and I couldn't afford to have a day off!

11

THINGS SEEMS TO GET BETTER ~ BUT DO THEY?

Over the next month, Jonna seemed to improve
somewhat. She even started making some meals.
Even though she was not much of a cook, I gave her
lots of encouragement. Her mood swings were still
happening but not quite as extreme as they were in
the beginning. Her addiction to the Head-X tablets
was getting worse. Sometimes she would pop 8 in a
day, even though I told her the directions said,
DANGER - Do not exceed the recommended dose.

Towards the end of the week, I had 4 bills to pay as
well as the rent. I was near enough to broke without
actually being penniless. Even though I made, what
was considered to be, good money at the time, with
only one person working it didn't go very far.
Friday morning, before my going to work, she asked
me for cigarette money. When I told her that I only
had enough for a bacon sandwich at the Foundry
lunch service, she lost it! Big Time! I rolled her 3
home-made fags and put them on the table.
"This no fucking good. Me need my cigarettes, not
yours. Me need 'Hoypin' (headache) tablets. No
more left!"
"I don't have any money for Head-X and smokes til
I get home this afternoon." Now she was really
pissed! I decided to leave for work before a full-
blown drama hit the fan. When I returned home in
the afternoon, after getting paid, I gave her a week's
worth of food money and enough for smokes and

Head-X tablets. Without any warning, she took the 1-pound bills from me, grabbed the lighter and set them on fire!

"Ya fucking, crazy bitch!" I yelled as I made a dive for the money which now had flames coming off of them. In the process of trying to get the money out of her hand, she stumbled on the floor, squashing the bills between my hands. I managed to put the flames out but not before half of them were destroyed.

"You bastard!" she said as she sat on the floor, throwing a tantrum. "You hurt my wrist, is sore!"

"What the fuck is the matter with you? I worked my arse off all week, in a stinking Foundry, for that money and you set it on fire! Why?"

"You no leave me money for cigarettes and 'Hoypin' tablets, you bastard man!"

"You know what Jonna, you're fucking lucky you're with me. Another man would have knocked you arse over head!"

"You no give cigarettes." She yelled.

"I had no fucking money this morning. Are you that fucking stupid ya can't understand that?" I said.

"You no give cigarettes, you no get sex!"

This threat of hers caused me to laugh as I said "I don't hardly get any now so what difference will that make?"

"You no get more."

"Let me make this easy for you to understand Jonna. Ya pussy is close to your arse so why don't you stick it up there and see if I care and while we're at it, Fuck you Bitch, I'm going out!"

"Where you go?"

"Sowerby Bridge Market to get some food with what's left of the money, before it closes."

70

"You bring me fucking cigarette and 'Hoypin' tablets."
"Fuck you ya bitch." I said as I walked out the door.

WHAT NOW YORKY MATE!

Walking down the road to the market, I was at my wits end. 'What the fuck am I going to do with her?' If I thought my life had taken a turn for the worse, this latest bullshit was nothing in comparison to what was going to happen in the future. It was just as well I was not a psychic and couldn't read the future. 'Why don't you hit the bitch on the head with a claw hammer and bury her in the back garden somewhere? You've killed lots of animals in the Bush before.'
"Don't be so fucking stupid." I said to the voice. "If I thought I could get away with it, I'd put her out of her misery but the chances are I'd get caught and end up swinging from a fucking rope."

That idea was a catalyst for an old memory to come surging up from the murky depths. As a boy, I used to do anything I could to get my father's attention, which I craved. Once I'd pissed him off enough, he said to my mother, "That bloody son of yours is going to end up dancing on the end of a rope, one of these days."
The next voice that spoke out, on the stage of the mind, said to me, 'Well, there's one thing for sure. you can't give her a week's food money anymore 'cause as soon as she gets the shits, she'll piss it away on headache tablets or send it up in smoke again.' This time I was in complete agreement with the voice. I worked really hard for that money and couldn't afford for that to happen again.

SERIOUS TIMES

Sad to say, my relationship with Jonna did not improve much at all. Everything about it hinged on her massive mood swings. By the time she was seven months pregnant, she still refused to go to the doctors for a checkup. Every time I brought the subject up, it always ended the same way, in a drama until the one day she said to me, "I need doctor, me bleeding." The fact that she asked for a doctor when she had been so adamant about not seeing one for the whole of her pregnancy, caused me some concern. I took off across the street to a telephone box that was just up the road aways.

When the doctor arrived, a quick checkup confirmed that unless Jonna went to the hospital immediately, she was in grave danger of losing the baby. Had it been me who told Jonna she needed to go to the hospital, I would have been the biggest bastard under the sun but this old doctor carried a great deal of authority. I never heard a squeak out of her. In fact, she looked really worried. I quickly packed an overnight bag for her with some things she would need for a few days stay. It didn't take long for the ambulance to arrive and once Jonna was comfortably laid down on a stretcher, the ambulance took off for the Halifax Infirmary.

When the ambulance was out of sight, I went back inside mi cottage made a cup of instant coffee for a change. Sitting in front of the fire, which was

constantly on during the winter months, I rolled a
smoke and sipped on the hot coffee. By this time, I
had gotten used to the idea of Jonna having a baby
even though it was impossible to tell as she never
gained more than a couple of pounds weight.
Visually, nothing showed.

At the Foundry, I worked two shifts. One week was
6 to 2 in the afternoon and the following week was 2
to 10 at night. This week was the afternoon shift so I
planned on going to the infirmary to visit Jonna
early the next morning as I would be back in time
for work.

I left the cottage early and caught a double-decker to
Halifax. The bus stopped pretty close to the
infirmary. After a short walk through the sludge and
snow, I stood at the reception desk.
"I'm here to see Jonna Jensen. She was brought in
yesterday."
"Let me find out where she is sir. Do you know it's
not visiting hours right?"
"No, I have no idea what time visiting hours are."

Once we found out which ward Jonna was in, the
receptionist told me I'd have to come back at 2
o'clock. "I can't do that. I have to be at work at 2."
"Let me call one of the Sisters. She may be able to
make an exception for you."
The Sister was a very kind, middle-aged woman
who understood that I would need time off work to
visit so she made an exception based on my work
hours.
"Before you go in to visit your wife, I'd like you to

74

see the Doctor. He can explain Jonna's condition to you." The Doctor was a middle-aged, matter of fact, no bullshit sort of bloke who asked me quite a lot of questions about Jonna's life style and background.

"What's the problem with her Doc? Why did she start bleeding?" I asked.
"We're not sure yet but let me ask you, are you still having sex together?" This question almost caused me to laugh. "No Doc, sex in my relationship is like 'rocking-horse shit!"
"I beg your pardon?" said the Doctor.
"Just joking Doctor. It's a source of drama between us."
"We did a blood test on her and found an unusual amount of drugs in her system, the type used in headache treatment."
"That's probably 'cause she's addicted to Head-X tablets. She takes 8, sometimes 10 a day."
"Is this another one of your jokes?"
"Not this time Doc."
"Oh my! That is not good at all. I will need to speak to her about that. It's probably why the baby is under-sized. How long has she been pregnant, would you say?"
"Seven months, give or take a week."
"That's not possible. She's way too small for seven months."
"I'm quite sure it's 7 months 'cause that's when we met. So, when can she come home?"
"Come home? She can't go home, unless she wants to lose the baby. She hasn't been looking after herself well enough. We'll have to keep her in the Infirmary until she has the baby. I take it she smokes

as well?"

"Yeah Doc."

"How many?"

"Twenty a day."

"Twenty a day, in her condition? Well, that won't be happening while she's under our care. Doesn't she have any family over here?"

"No Doc, just me."

"Look, this is the bottom line. If we let her go home, she'll lose the baby for sure. She needs complete bed rest until she gives birth."

"Ya mean, she'll be in here for 2 months?"

"At least, maybe 3."

'What a bloody ripper', I thought but decided not to voice it. "Can I see her?"

"Yes, but she won't be very responsive. I've put her on a mild sedative to keep her quiet as she seems to be quite volatile."

"I know what you mean Doc."

"Also, her language leaves a lot to be desired. You may need to have a chat with her about it."

"Is that it Doc?"

"That's it for now, although there is one last thing. If she's been taking as many of these strong headache pills, as you say, there is a possibility that the child will be a bit slow."

"Ya mean a retard!"

"Well, I wouldn't quite put it that way, I prefer the word 'slow' myself."

"Anything else, while we're at it?"

"No, I think that about covers everything, except try not to let her get over-excited or emotional when you visit her."

"Suppose she does, then what?"

"Probably better to just quietly leave and come back at another time."

"Thanks very much for your honesty and time Doc. I really appreciate it."

"And don't you worry yourself, lots of women go through this with their first pregnancy."

When I found Jonna, she was in a room with three other women. She was laid in bed with a drip in her arm which I presumed was to give her or the baby extra nourishment as the Doctor said they were both underweight. Her eyes were closed when I sat down at her bedside, so I just sat there for a while looking at her. In the short time I had known Jonna, I had never seen her looking so peaceful. She almost looked Angelic. When I gently touched her arm, she slowly opened her eyes.

"How are ya love?" I asked.

Once she was fully awake, she said "Me no good. They put me to sleep and stick this thing in my arm."

"The Doctor says you're underweight and so is the baby."

"Me no care. Me come home tomorrow."

"Jonna, I think you need to understand something. The Doctor said you will have to stay in the Infirmary until you have the baby or it will fall out."

"Me no stay in Hospital. Me come home tomorrow."

As gently as I could, I explained to Jonna everything the Doctor told me and that he would not sign her out of the infirmary because, for sure, she would lose the baby. Tears started to well up in her eyes now as she lay there in a helpless state.

"Is your fault me pregnant! Me no want fucking baby. Me want to go home."
"I'm sorry Jonna, there's nothing I can do about it. You're under the Doctors care now."
"You bring me cigarette."
"Can't do that. You can only smoke outside and the Doctor says you need to rest for the next eight weeks."

Once Jonna realized she would not be coming home in a few days, she really started to get upset. I called the Ward Sister who came in to try and calm her down.
"Maybe you'd better go." she said to me. "Until she gets used to the idea that she can't go home 'til she's given birth."
"Don't worry Jonna, I'll come back and visit you tomorrow at the same time." with that said, I left her in the capable hands of the Ward Sister.

As the days went by, it became increasing obvious that Jonna would not be coming home again until she gave birth. It was not easy for her and at the same time it was not very easy for me. I visited her every day until she had the baby. Well, near enough every day. Some days, when I visited, she would be fine and at other times she would be depressed which manifested in anger towards me. At those times she would tell me to fuck off and not bother coming to visit. When that happened, I would take a day off from visiting, as it was a three-mile bus ride to the Infirmary. When I was on the afternoon shift, I would have to get two separate buses and go straight to work until 10 at night.

The good thing about Jonna being in the Infirmary was my life had reverted back to what it was before I met her. The weeks that I was on the morning shift, I would visit her in the afternoon, which meant the evenings were all mine. I took the opportunity to get out to the local Pub with some of my old school chums and make the best if it while I still could. I even went hunting rabbits with my mate Jim, on a Sunday morning, which I absolutely loved!

Steve, a great school friend of mine, whose place I had stayed at when I first came back to England for a visit, said to me, "Hey Dick Lad, have ya got all the baby stuff for when ya girlfriend comes home?"
"No mate, not yet. Why?"
"Well, don't go buying anything now, 'cause I've got everything you'll need in mi back shed."
"Is it in good shape Steve?"
"Yeah Dick, It's like brand new. It was only used for a couple of months before mi missus decided she had to have something better than the next-door neighbor. The cot hasn't got a mark on it and the pram is not the latest model but it's clean and in good shape."
"I'll take it Steve. How much d'ya want for it."
"Now't Dick Lad, consider it a gift."
"Are ya sure? I can give ya a few quid for it?"
"Wouldn't dream of it Dick Lad. In fact, I'll be glad to get it out of mi shed. Then I can start using it as a potting shed again."
The cot and pram were just as Steve had described. All I needed now were blankets, clothes and the rest of the paraphernalia it takes to keep a baby alive.

79

Finally, the big day arrived! The Doctor, who was looking after Jonna, could not believe it when the Sister told him she was ready to give birth. The last time I had visited Jonna, the Sister told me to ring the infirmary before coming in just in case she was in the Delivery Room.

I was on the morning shift at work so I spent my evening having a couple of beers with my rabbit hunting mate, Jim. I called the Infirmary every hour, after 6 o'clock to see if there was any change in Jonna's condition. Finally, at almost closing time, the receptionist told me, I was the father of a brand-new baby boy!
"Can I come in and see them both?" I asked.
"It's better if you come in tomorrow morning or afternoon as Jonna had been given a strong sedative so she could sleep. Apparently, she had a rough time of it."
When I told mi mate Jim, he said, "Congratulations Dick Lad. At least you got a boy. I'm stuck with three fucking girls! Ya know what that means, right? Soon as they're old enough to start going out with boys, they'll be bringing their fucking problems home with them." We had a couple more beers before the Landlord called 'Time'. The Landlord even shouted me a beer, once he heard the news.

WHAT NOW?

That evening, drinking a beer and puffing away on a cigarette, I sat in front of the fire contemplating what my life was going to be like as I was now a father to another human being. What if he's 'slow' like the Doctor said. Worst case scenario, what if he's a fucking retard from all the headache tablets she took. I wonder if Jonna's going to be any different, now she's a new mother or if having a baby to look after is going to make her worse. I've heard some people say a new baby brought couples together, while others said it amplified their problems and made their relationship worse. These were a few of the thoughts that swirled around my mind as I sat there. After the beer was gone and the smoke was burnt out, I had no more answers than when I first sat down. "Fuck it!", I said out loud. I turned off the fire and then took miself off to bed. Tomorrow's another day!

That evening was a very cold one. I hopped into bed and pulled the blankets up as fast as possible. As I lay there, in the darkness, I started to remember what my life was like, growing up in the Outback of Australia. In those days, I felt like I was in complete control of my life. If I didn't want to work, I didn't. I was only responsible for miself. I could go wherever I wanted, whenever I wanted. Now look at the state that I'm in. I'm stuck in a shit-hole called England. I've got a girlfriend living with me who's as crazy as a cut snake and the icing on the cake is, I just found out that I'm a father! Where's the control in that? I felt like a prisoner who had just been handed down a 20 year sentence.

~15~

SEEING MY SON FOR THE FIRST TIME

Standing at the side of Jonna's bed, I smiled at her
and said, "So you did it Jonna. Ya got through it all
right?"
The first words out of her mouth were, "I had a
fucking boy!"
I couldn't believe it. The first words out of her
mouth, 'I had a fucking boy!'
"Jonna, that's really great. Have you seen him yet?"
"Yes, but me no want to see him. I no want a boy.
Me want a girl. I no like have a fucking boy!"

Right at that moment a ward nurse came into the
room and said to me, "Have you seen your son yet?"
"No, I just got here."
"Oh, well, let me take you to see him."
"Thanks nurse, that sounds great."

Once we were in the nursery, I saw that there were
eight small cots with babies in them and two that
were in what, I thought, looked like two fish tanks
with a small baby in each one.
"This is your son." said the nurse as she pointed to
one of the incubators. "He's extremely underweight
so he will have to say in the incubator until he's
heavy enough to go home."
I was absolutely stunned when I saw him lying
there. He had a tube in his arm and one in his leg.
He also had a monitoring wire and a patch on his
heart area. He had a thin covering of blonde hair,
blue eyes and was quite long. His arms and legs

83

were so skinny, he looked a bit like a skeleton covered in skin.

"Is he going to live?" was the first thing I asked the nurse.

"Oh yes, it's going to take a while for him to gain weight but he's going to be fine."

"So why is he so thin?"

"Well, according to the Doctor who checked him out, your wife didn't take real good care of herself. That's why we insisted she stay in the infirmary. She would have probably lost him if not."

"How heavy does he have to be before he can go home?"

"Five and a half pounds."

"How long will that take?"

"I'd say about 4 or 5 weeks."

"How much does he way now?"

"Three pounds one ounce."

"That's not very much is it?"

"No, but we've had smaller babies than him in here and they've grown up to be normal and healthy. Let me show you something." The nurse walked over to the other incubator. "This little girl is only two pounds 7 ounces. She was born premature. She was only in the womb for seven months."

"Will she make it?" I asked.

"Yes, as long as there are no major complications."

Back at my son's incubator, I said to the nurse, "Why does he need those tubes in his arms and legs?"

"He needs special nourishment as baby formula will not be enough for him to gain weight and his mother cannot provide enough milk for him so we're feeding him intravenously."

"You're sure he's going to live?"

"Oh yes, he's going to be fine. Once he's running around and into everything he can get his hands on, you won't remember him being so small."

"Can I come and visit him every day?"

"Sure, once he's taking a bottle, you can have a go at feeding him."

"Thanks so much nurse." I said as we left the nursery.

"Oh, don't mention it. It's my pleasure. That's why I do this work."

Back at Jonna's bedside, the nurse had put the flowers I brought into a vase of water on her bedside table.

"He's really beautiful Jonna. He's got a thin covering of blonde hair and blue eyes, but he's a bit skinny so he will have to stay here until he's five and a half pounds."

"I no want a fucking boy, I want a girl!" and with that said, she started to cry.

"Don't cry." I said. "Everything will be alright."

"Not alright! Me want a girl!"

"Did it hurt having him?"

"No, me get needle 'cause I don't want baby." I did my best to comfort her but the more I tried the worse I seemed to make it.

"All right Jonna, I'm gonna' leave now. I'll come again tomorrow. Do you need me to bring you anything?"

"Me want fucking cigarette." she said, between sobs.

"I'll ask the nurse before I leave alright?"

"Me want to go home."

"I'll ask the Doctor or the Nurse when you can get out of here. It shouldn't be much longer now that you've had him."

Once I found the ward Nurse, I asked her about smokes for Jonna and she said, "She should be able to go outside and sit in a chair on the lawn tomorrow. We allow smoking out there."

I explained to the nurse that Jonna didn't want a boy, she wanted a girl.

"She has post-partum depression." (Whatever the fuck that is.) I asked her why Jonna takes so many headache tablets.

"Does she have some kind of problem?" I asked.

"No, she doesn't. She kept asking for headache tables when she was first admitted so the Doctor gave her an extensive examination and as far as he's concerned, there's nothing wrong with Jonna."

"So why is she always complaining of headaches and popping headache tablets?"

"The Doctor says she's addicted to them. He explained to Jonna that they're not good for her, especially in large doses. If I were you, I'd try your best to keep her off of them as the one's that she's been taking are not very good for the liver."

"How about the depression? Will she get over that soon?"

"It's hard to say. It takes some women longer than others. The Doctor will want to have a chat with you before he lets her go home. He feels that Jonna has a lot of emotional issues from her childhood that need taking care of, but he'll go into that in more detail when you see him."

Sitting on the top deck of the bus, I rolled a smoke and watched the scenery go by, as had been my habit for the past eight weeks. Jonna was probably coming home in the next couple of days. My son would not be coming home for another month or so, which meant that I would have another month or so of traveling back and forth to the infirmary. (Jonna would not go to see him at all.)

Finally, the day came when we could pick up our son. Jonna had been home for a month and surprisingly she had been in good spirits. She was, what I would call, normal, which to me meant no crazy high drama. Although it came pretty close to that as we went back and forth choosing a name for him. Eventually we settled on the name Anthony Craig, which we were both happy with, wonder of wonders.

The nurses who had looked after him were quite sad to see him go. They had grown quite fond of him as he had spent so much time with them.
"Well. here he is." said the nurse. "He's all yours now. Make sure you look after him." she said as she handed him to Jonna.
"He's a beautiful, well-behaved baby. He sleeps really well between bottles. Have you picked out a name for him yet?"
"Yes, Anthony Craig."
"Oh that's a lovely name. He actually looks like an 'Anthony'."
The nurse then proceeded to give me all the information we would need to look after him as regards baby formula and how often he feeds etc.

She also told us a district nurse would call on us once a week for the first month to keep a check on him seeing as he was so small at birth and once every 6 weeks thereafter. That was about it.
"Jonna, you're very fortunate you have a beautiful baby boy there so look after him and make sure you look after yourself love." said the nurse.

On the bus ride home at least 4 women passengers asked if they could see his face as he was so bundled up. Every one of them said something like, "Oh isn't she a lovely little girl."
"How old is she?"
"One month." I said "and he's a boy, not a girl!"
"Oh, I'm sorry love. He's so beautiful I just presumed he was a girl."
I never let the possibility of having a good joke escape me, so I said, "It's because he looks like me that he's so handsome, don't ya think?" Without a doubt, everyone agreed and then added, "But we can't forget his mother, can we? She's also a beautiful girl." This little comment made Jonna smile, which considering all she had been through these past months was a pleasure to see.

Once we arrived home Jonna put him in a carry-cot next to the fire to keep him warm as the room could get quite cold on the days when what bit of sun there was merged behind big fluffy snow clouds. As I watched her tuck him into the cot, I reminded myself to keep a bit of an eye on her as I knew how unstable she could be. Any little thing could set her off.

Over the next few weeks the nurse's words proved to be true. Anthony was a wonderful baby. According to the nurse, he was supposed to be fed every four hours but sometimes he would sleep for six hours straight with not a peep out him. Sometimes I got a bit worried about him and would check to see if he was still alive. The district nurse would show up once a week as scheduled to make sure he was healthy. At those times, I asked her many questions about the best ways to look after a baby.

"Should we wake him up for a feed if he sleeps over four hours?"

"No, when he's sleeping, he's growing. Just feed him when he wakes up."

At first, I was a bit frightened of holding him as I'd never been around babies before. Most of my working life was spent dragging out 150 pound sheep all day. I wasn't sure if he'd break or snap in two, seeing as he was so bendy. I even learned how to change his shitty nappies without sticking the safety pin into his belly. I must admit, the smell of shit and ammonia was a bit hard to tolerate at first but like most things in life that are necessary, I soon learned to accept.

My mother, who was in the process of selling her house so she could move to Cleethorpes, would come and visit every now and then which was a great help to me but not to Jonna who felt that she was being critical the way mi mother offered her advice. After having 3 children of her own she felt qualified to give advice. One day, when mi mother offered her some useful information, Jonna got the shits big time and told mi mother to piss off, "He's my baby, not yours! I look after him like I want to not how you want to!" Well, that was it. That was the last I saw of mi mother. A few weeks later she had moved to her new house by the seaside.

As the weeks rolled by, Jonna started to slip back into her old ways. Once again, her habit of popping headache tablets re-emerged. At those times, she would lay around in bed or on the couch and refuse to take care of Anthony. Obviously, I got the shits myself as I had to look after him and still get up at 5 in the morning to go to the Foundry.

During the week, I would leave Jonna with enough money for the day's food and a pack of smokes. Each time I did this, she would first buy her fags and Head-Ex tablets. Whatever money that was leftover, she'd buy food with which meant half the things we needed were missing. In the end, I made sure there was enough food in the house and only left enough money for a packet of smokes which, of course, created a huge drama!

On one particular occasion, when I got home from work, she had the shits big time. Anthony was laid in his cot and his nappies hadn't been changed for hours.
"Why haven't you changed his nappy Jonna? I can smell him from here."
"Me got no cigarettes or 'hoypin' (headache) tablets."
"You had a full pack of smokes when I left this

morning. What happened to them?"

"No more 'hoypin' tablets so me smoke them all."

"What's that got to do with changing Anthony's nappy? If you don't change it when it gets full, he'll get a big rash on his arse."

"Fuck you Richard! You change him! No 'hoypin' tablets, I no look after him. He's your son, you look after him."

"Jonna, you can't behave like this anymore. When the District Nurse comes for a visit, if she sees Anthony's not being cared for properly, she'll take him away from us and stick him in a home where he will be looked after!"

"I no care. No cigarettes and 'hoypin' tablets and I no look after him!"

That was it! I'd been working really hard at the Foundry since Anthony had been home, because of all the extra things that had to be bought for a new baby. I said to Jonna, "Then fuck you, ya fucking Danish bitch! Ya don't want to look after him then you get no more cigarettes until ya do!" That bit of information pushed her right over the top. She screamed a mixture of English and Danish obscenities at me and then rushed out of the house. Then I heard the sound of breaking glass. The bitch had picked up the washing prop and smashed both of the sash windows. There was glass all over the chairs and carpet. The cold wind and snow was now being blown inside the cottage room. By this time, Anthony was crying his eyes out as he had no idea what the hell was happening. 'Jesus fucking christ', I thought. 'What the fucking hell do I do now?' Jonna continued to scream her head off, outside in the snow. I only had three neighbors and all of them opened their doors to find out what the screaming and broken glass was all about. Once she had stopped yelling and screaming, she came inside, put her hat, coat and boots on and walked out the door and slammed it behind her. That was the last I saw of her til around 9 o'clock that night.

The next time the District Nurse came calling, I had a good talk with her in private and made her aware of all the nonsense and dramas that were going on. I suggested to her that she have a talk with Jonna about her behavior and that if it didn't change, she could threaten her with the child welfare people taking Anthony into protective custody.
The District Nurse was a kind-hearted lady and she agreed with me 100%, but it didn't change Jonna's attitude very much. After ten days or so, she was up to her old habits again. On one occasion, on our once-a-week trip to Halifax to buy the weeks food supply, we were walking around the shops. Stopping outside a young women's clothing store, Jonna saw a designer dress that she really wanted.
"Look at that sexy dress Richard. Me want that dress!"
"It's too expensive Jonna. I paid all the bills this week and we've only got enough money left for food and smokes."
"I don't care! Me want it. Me go in shop and try it on."

The shop girl found Jonna the right size and she disappeared into the changing room to try it on. When she came back out, she said, "Look Richard,

is good size for me and is really sexy-looking!"
"Yeah, it is Jonna but I told you already, we don't have that kind of money. Why would you want a sexy dress when you're as cold as a dead fish?"
"Fuck you Richard, you bastard! You fucking go shopping on your own. Me go home!"
With that said, she took off the dress and put her own clothes back on and started to walk out of the shop.
"What about Anthony? Take him home with you!"
"Fuck you!" she shouted. "You take him home!"

As I was walking out of the shop, I said to the girl, "The dress is in the changing room love."
"I guess you won't be buying it?" she asked with an embarrassed look on her face. "Sorry I couldn't help you."
"Don't be sorry love, it's not your fault."
Back outside the shop, Jonna was nowhere to be seen. I made sure Anthony's blankets were tucked in and took off for the food market. Coming back from Halifax on the bus, on my own, with Anthony was not the easiest thing to do. Saturday afternoon was a shopping day for most people and the busses tended to be quite full. In order to get on the bus, I first had to put two heavy shopping bags on the platform first. Then I had to take Anthony out of the push-chair, hold him in one arm and at the same time, do my best to fold up the push-chair. In those days, the busses had a driver and a conductor. Lucky for me, the conductor was a woman who I knew from traveling on her bus many times before. "Can I hold your baby for you while you collapse the pushchair?"

"That would be great love, thanks a lot."
I stowed the shopping bags and pushchair in the luggage compartment under the stairs which was not easy as many other passengers had done the same thing. Anthony was quiet as a mouse in the Conductress' arms as he stared into her eyes.
"Oh my God." she said to me. "His eyes as so clear and blue, it feels like he can see right through me!"
"Do you have any children?"
"No, I never found the right man."
"Well, maybe that's a blessing in disguise. They're very confronting things these babies. Once you've got one, there's no sending them back."

Once I reached my stop, outside Cavendish Buildings, The Conductress helped me off with the shopping bags and the pushchair. She even figured out how to open it up and push the two safety rings down on the handle.
'Thanks love." I said as she pushed the bell and the Double-Decker slowly pulled away from the curb.

Once I had Anthony in the house, I put him on a blanket, a safe distance from the fire and then I brought the groceries inside and last of all, the pushchair. It took me quite a while to warm up the water and give him a bath. After that little job was done, I put a clean nappy on and bedtime clothes on him. I fed him a small jar of baby food which he got all over himself. By the time I had finished there was more food in his hair and on his clothes than had gone in his mouth. His favorite trick was to blurt the food out all over me. I had gone through his feeding regime many times before so I was already prepared. I had a big tea towel, tucked inside the top of mi jumper, that hung down the front of mi clothes. When I was finished, I wasn't sure who was the baby, him or me, as we were both covered in food.

NEXT!

Anthony was now 11 months old and growing quite well, to say he was only three pounds at birth and considering he was a very fussy eater. Jonna had a crazy idea that small babies should not be allowed to crawl around on the floor and pull themselves up on the furniture lest they put sticky finger marks on it. Another bit of madness, Anthony was not allowed to eat brown chocolate in case he got dirty. White chocolate was all he could eat.

Every day when I got home from work, I would find Anthony sitting up in a high chair and was not allowed out of it. I asked Jonna how long he'd been in the chair. She said "All day. He make mess of the furniture and me have to clean up and polish everything again." This neurosis of Jonna's carried on for almost 5 weeks until I got sick of it as it was retarding his growth. I must admit to my part in the situation as I didn't want to cause another high drama. I kept quiet about it until one day I could keep quiet no more.

I was on the morning shift, which meant that I was home around 3 o'clock. Anthony was sat in his high chair crying and Jonna was stretched out on the couch smoking a fag.
"Has Anthony been out of his high chair today?" I asked.
"No, he make big mess and me have to clean up!" That statement pushed me over the top! I walked over to the high chair and took him out of it. I gave him a cuddle until he stopped crying. Once he was

smiling at my pulling funny faces with mi top false teeth, I put him on the carpet and said "There ya go mate. Have fun!"

All the while, Jonna was watching us and as soon as I went upstairs to change out of mi work clothes, she picked him up and put him back in the high chair. What did I do? I did what I should have done a month ago. I picked Anthony up out of the chair and put him back down on the carpet.
"He not allowed on carpet. He make messy everything!"
"I don't care how much mess he makes; you can't keep him in that high chair forever! He needs to crawl around and pull himself up on everything so he can learn to walk."
"Is alright for you. Me have to clean up and polish furniture from finger marks!"
With that, she picked up Anthony and put him back in the high chair.
"Your days of keeping him stuck in that high chair are over and if you persist in putting him back in when I've taken him out of it, I'll chop the bloody thing into pieces. Then there'll be no high chair left to put him in!"

What came next was beyond my imagination. She got up off of the couch and took Anthony out of the high chair while screaming obscenities at me. Then she walked into the kitchen while still holding Anthony and took the butchers knife out of the drawer. When she walked back into the main room, she held the butcher's knife to Anthony's throat and said, "You fucking bastard Richard! You no tell me what to do with my baby or I cut his fucking throat!"

This act of insanity got my attention, big time.

"Come on Jonna, don't be so fucking stupid! Put the knife down."

"Fuck you Richard, he's my baby. I do what I want with him!"

I took two steps towards her and said "Give me the knife or put it down."

"Fuck you!" she said and took a swing at me with the knife.

I got such a shock that I jumped back three feet and almost fell over an armchair.

"Don't be so bloody stupid! Put the knife down or I'll call the police."

"You call! I no care. He my baby. I get my mother to send me money. I go back to Denmark and take Anthony with me."

"Alright, no problem. Just put the knife down!"

"Fuck you Bastard. You no take him out of high chair anymore."

"Alright Jonna, are you gonna put the knife down or not?"

"No, he my baby. He sit in high chair."

There was no other option left for me so I said again "I'm going to call the cops now."

"I no care what you do."

By this time, she had worked herself up into quite a frenzy as she still held the knife dangerously close to Anthony's throat. I put on mi coat and boots and headed for the pay phone across the street. 999 was a free call so I dialed the number. I had never dialed the emergency number before and was surprised how fast they responded.

"Emergency, which service do you require?"

"Police please."

"What's it about?"

"My girlfriend is threatening to kill my son with a knife!"

"What's your address sir?"

After giving her my name and address, she said, "We're sending someone out straight away!"

Once I was back in the cottage, Jonna was still pacing around the room with the knife in one hand and Anthony in her arm, still crying.

"You'd better put the knife down; the police are on their way."

"You liar Richard. You no call police."

"I'm not lying, they're on the way."

Sowerby Bridge Police Station was at the bottom of Sowerby New Road so it was only a matter of minutes before there was a loud knocking on the door. Jonna held the knife closer to Anthony's throat as she realized I was not lying.

When I opened the door, there was a big, portly sergeant and a young, skinny constable stood there with very serious looks on their faces. As I closed the door behind me the older sergeant said, "You called 999? What's the emergency?"

"My girlfriends inside holding our baby and she's got a butchers knife to his throat and threatening to kill him. She's just gone nuts 'cause I keep taking him out of his high chair."

99

"Why are ya doing that?"

" 'Cause he's never allowed out of it in case he messes the room up."

"No problem. I'll handle the situation from here on."

The sergeant walked into the room and I went to follow him inside. He said to me, "It's better that you stay outside with my constable. Your presence may antagonize the situation. This shouldn't take long."

The sergeant closed the door behind him and the young constable and myself tried to look through the lace-curtained window. The door had not closed properly and was open about four inches. It was not too hard to hear what was going on.

Walking towards Jonna, the sergeant said, "Now what seems to be the problem here young lady? Put the knife down."

Jonna took a step towards him and said, "Fuck off fat pig!" She took a swing at him with the knife.

"Whoa, steady on!" he said. "Nobody's going to hurt you."

"Get out my fucking house bastard!"

"Alright love, I'm going outside for a few minutes but I want you to settle down and put the knife away." With that said, the sergeant quickly left the room.

Standing outside again he said, "This is a bit more serious than I thought it would be. I'm going to have to re-think the situation! Has she been like this before?"

"Not this bad. She's never threatened my son like this before, although she once threw a knife at me

when she lost it but it missed and hit the wall."
"Right then, I think the best approach would be to try and calm her down before getting the knife away from her."

With that said, he went back into the room, a bit more slowly this time. Standing outside in the freezing cold weather, I said to the constable, "Are you married?"
"No, but I've got a long-term girlfriend. We're saving up for the deposit before we take the plunge."
"I trust she's a bit more stable than my girlfriend."
"Oh aye, she's a couple of years older than me and she's got a good head on her shoulders. She's college educated, in fact, she even makes more money than me."
"Well, that's great. I'm happy for ya. It sounds like you'll never have a problem like I've got."
"I hope not. She's a good lass, is my Sarah."

It took the sergeant about half an hour before he persuaded Jonna to hand over the knife. When he came back outside, he said, "That was a bit touch and go there for a while but I think she's pretty calm now. She's not a very stable lass ya know. You might consider getting her some professional help."
"I've tried that but she won't see anyone and I can't force her."
"She doesn't seem to want the lad crawling around the place which can't be too healthy for him."
"That's what the big drama was about. I threatened to chop up the high chair and she lost it!"
"Right. What about charges."
"What do you mean 'charges'?"

"By rights, you can file charges against her for endangering your son's life and I strongly suggest you do."

"If I do that sergeant, who's gonna look after my son when I go to work?"

"Don't ya have any relations that could look after him?"

"No, mi mother and sisters live miles away."

"Alright, then I understand but this is how it goes. If we're called out again to your place over a situation similar to this, it won't be up to you to press charges. We'll arrest her and have her committed to an institution where she can get the help she obviously needs. I've explained that to her, so she knows what will happen if we have to call here again."

Not long after the Police incident, Jonna's mental state had improved, slightly. That doesn't mean she was well, it just meant that her dramas didn't escalate enough for me to call the cops again.

Anthony was progressing really well at crawling around. He was already standing up whilst holding on to the furniture which was a joy for me to see. Around this time, I started thinking about buying a better house that had an inside toilet and constant hot water.

There was a mill at the bottom of Sowerby New Road called Eddlestons that had a nursery that would look after children for the mothers who wished to return to work. I made a few inquiries to find out all about it. The woman who was in charge of the nursery gave me a guided tour of the place and assured me that the children were well cared for. After a lot more thought about getting a better place to live, I decided to approach the idea with Jonna. When I brought the subject up, she lit up immediately and thought it was a good idea, until I told her "If I go ahead and do this, you will have to go back to work."

I explained to her about Eddlestons looking for trained weavers. Having a nursery for the children meant I wouldn't have to pay a lot of money for private child care. Once I told her about the perks of a place with an inside toilet, constant hot water and central heating, she agreed to do it.
The one thing I made sure she fully understood was that my wages alone were not enough to take on a mortgage and if she got the shits and refused to keep working I would sell the place and buy another cheap house.

At that time, the Halifax Building Society was offering 100% free deposit for first time home buyers. After discussing my financial income with one of their agents, he assured me that I qualified for a mortgage up to 4,000 pounds. With that bit of positive information, I started reading the local newspaper ads and real estate offerings.

It didn't take long to find a great 2-bedroom semi-detached house at a place called Pye Nest Road. The asking price was 4,200 pounds, which was more money than the Building Society would loan me. After explaining my situation with the current owners, they agreed to drop the price to 3,800 pounds, if I was serious, which I was. The Building Society said it would take a month or so for the mortgage to go through. In the meantime, I tested out Jonna's promise to go back to work. She actually went to the Mill to apply for a job on her own, with Anthony. Seeing as she was a trained weaver with previous experience, she was hired on the spot and told to start work on the following Monday. That was great news for me because now we could save enough money for some better furniture and whatever extra expenses came up.

She was not thrilled about getting up early in the morning and making breakfast for herself and Anthony, who was now walking around on his own, but she was doing it so I gave her lots of praise and encouragement, as she was a lot like a child herself.

Eventually, the day came when we were given the go-ahead by the Building Society to move in. Before leaving 8 Cavendish Buildings, a young single-mother came to see me about renting the place. Her brother had been in my class at school so I had met her before, at their parents' house. She explained to me that after she had the baby her boyfriend dumped her and done a runner. She was left to fend for herself and the baby and was at present back home, living in her parent's place. Me, being the soft-hearted man that I was, I gave her the place for free, on the condition that she keep up the payments so nothing would backfire on me. Once I told her the deal, she agreed to it and was as happy as a pig in shit.

17

LIFE'S LOOKING UP?

For a while, my life looked like it was improving. I
was now part owner, with the Building Society, of a
really well-built, red brick, semi-detached house.
The bus stop to Halifax was only a few yards from
my front door. I had a front lawn which I kept in
good order and even planted a border of roses,
which looked beautiful while looking out of the
front window. At the back of house was a fairly
large block of land that I sowed down into another
lawn so Anthony would have a great place to play,
once the weather was warm enough. I even had a
one car garage that I could turn into a work shop for
miself, seeing as I couldn't afford a car, as they were
expensive to run in England, in those days.

I even bought a black and white TV for Jonna,
thinking that if she had some entertainment it would
keep her mind occupied and she didn't sink into
depression. The problem with the television was that
it didn't take very long for Jonna and Anthony to
become addicted to it to the point that I didn't even
exist anymore. Manys the time I regretted buying it.
It didn't take Anthony very long to learn how to
switch it on and turn the channel knob to a different
station. I'm not saying that I never watched it,
because I did. I liked watching music programs like
The Old Gray Whistle Test and Top of the Pops but
it caused more problems than it was worth. At a
pinch, I could have got rid of it in a heartbeat.

Anthony was now talking quite a bit. The problem was that he spoke 'pigeon' English, the same as his mother which was not surprising, under the circumstances. The first word he learned to say besides mum and dad was NO! Just like his mother, he used it at every opportunity.

One evening, I happened to be watching an interesting documentary when Anthony decided it wasn't what he wanted to watch. He walked over to the TV and turned the channel to another program and then sat down on the floor about two feet away from it.
"Anthony, turn the knob back to where it was."
"NO!" he said without even turning around.
This habit of his had become so bad in such a short time that something had to be done about it if I didn't want to watch Jinx the cat for the rest of mi life. I said again, "Anthony, turn the channel back to where it was and leave the TV alone."
As expected, his answer was a definite, NO!
"Alright mate, there is only one way you're gonna learn."
I got out of mi armchair, walked over to the TV and turned it off.
'That'll teach the little bugger', I thought to miself as I headed back to mi chair. Before mi arse was comfortably in mi chair, he had turned the TV back on. I got back up and turned it off again.
"Now leave it alone. I'm not telling you again.", I said, which was one of my mother's favorite lines.
No sooner was I sat down again, he said,
"NO" in a much louder voice and turned it on again.
"Alright mate, you asked for it."

I got out of mi chair again, turned off the TV, then pulled the plug out of the wall socket and returned to mi chair. Sitting there watching him closely, he turned the Off knob back on but the screen remained black.

'That fixed ya, ya little bugger.' I thought as I kept watching him.

In under a minute, he had crawled behind the TV which was placed in the corner. After a couple of tries he managed to put the plug into the wall socket and then turn the TV back on and shouted at me, "NO".

Jesus Christ, I thought to myself, he's becoming more like his mother every day! This calls for more drastic action. It was not my belief to spank children. It was better, as far as I'm concerned, to outsmart them. I had a bright idea. I went into the kitchen drawer and took out a pair of scissors. When I got back to the TV room, I walked up to the TV, turned it off, pulled the plug out of the wall. As Anthony sat there watching me, I made sure he could see what I was doing. Then I cut the plug off of the cord with the scissors and returned to my chair.

Anthony was no fool in those early days. He walked over to my chair and tried to take the plug out of my hand but I held on to it tight enough so he couldn't have it, otherwise he would've tried to plug it in again and possibly electrocute himself. Once he knew he was not getting the plug, he threw himself on the floor, in a tantrum more or less like his mother did.

Day by day, Jonna grew more discontented working

at the mill. She had been there for three months now. Anthony had progressed leaps and bounds from the interactions he had with the other children at the nursery, that is till one day when the shit hit the fan!

I had just got home from work, in the afternoon, when the woman who ran the nursery telephoned me.

"Regrettably, I can't allow Anthony to attend the nursery any more as he is very disruptive. He has started hitting the other children when he doesn't get his own way."

I thanked her for explaining Anthony's situation and then hung up the phone. 'Oh shit.', I thought. Now what do I do? He can't go back to the nursery anymore and there's no one else I know around this area who will baby sit for eight hours a day. Even if I could find someone I know, Jonna's going to use the situation as an excuse to stop working. Then how am I going to pay the mortgage and the bills which were at least double what they were at Cavendish Buildings?'

As expected, when Jonna and Anthony arrived home, she told me that the nursery woman had called her out of the mill to the nursery and explained the situation to her. True to form, she said, "I no work anymore. Nobody to look after Anthony and me sick of this job. It too hard!"

"I'll find someone around here to look after Anthony, then you don't have to stop working, or while I'm looking for another child-minder, you can look for another job." I told her.

"Me no look for other job. Me no like working

108

anymore."

After explaining to her that my work, as good as it was money-wise, was still not enough to pay the bills, long term. She still refused to go back to work or look for a better job.

"All right Jonna, this is the Johnny Dorry. I will look for a part-time job. I have no intentions of losing this house because I can't keep up with mortgage payments but as soon as 12 months are up, I'm putting it on the market for sale. We'll move back into a row house that I can afford to pay for on one wage."

"Me no moving! Me like this house."

"Well, you can keep thinking what you like but you'll end up very disappointed because I'm getting really fed up with your bullshit. I've done everything in my power to help you to have a good, happy life but as far as I can see, you're never going to be happy. Something in the near future has to be done because I'm not living like this anymore. If you don't want to live in a less-expensive house then I'll take you back to Denmark to live. You're always telling me how great Denmark is so you should be happy."

"Me no fucking go. Me stay here."

"Not if you don't go back to work. I've had enough of your nonsense to last me a bloody lifetime!"

Once it was obvious Jonna was not going to change her mind I thought to miself, 'Fuck this for a game of tin soldiers! I need to get away from this wench for a couple of hours or I'll end up doing something to her that I will regret.'

I put on mi hat and coat and headed for the door.

"Where you go Richard?"

"I'm off across the road for a couple of beers with mi mate Clint."
"You no have money for house but you have money for beer?"
"Fuck you, ya lying bitch." I said and walked out.

18

MAKING MUSIC

There was a great pub, about 200 yards from the house, that I used to retreat to every time Jonna pulled one of her stunts. Over the short time I'd lived at Pye Nest Road, I'd met some really decent people there. One man, in particular, was Clint. He lived closer to the pub than I did, in fact his house was about twenty feet away. Clint and I used to commiserate together as he had a wife and child and his marriage was just as bad as mine so we had a lot in common.

The pub was warm when I walked in and the vibe of the place was happy and friendly, which was more than I could say for my house. Clint was sat in the lounge finishing off a pint with a friend of his. I ordered a beer and made my way over to where he was sitting.

"Richard, how are are ya. Come and sit down with us."

"G'day Clint, how are ya mate?" I said.

"Oh, so so, ya know."

"Are ya sure ya won't have another pint Rex?" Clint said to his mate.

"Better not mate. I'm in the shit with mi old lady. She already thinks I spend too much time in here."

Once Rex had left, I bought Clint a pint and we sat there for a couple of hours swapping stories about our woeful home life. At one point Clint said to me, "By the way Richard, did I tell you mi good news?"

"What good news?"

"I went on an audition the other night to try out for playing rhythm guitar for a cabaret band, Dawn and the Daybreakers."

"Ya kidding mate. I didn't know you played guitar."

"Yeah, I haven't played in a band for about 15 years but I've still got mi Gibson 330 and an old Vox AC.30 amp."

"How did ya go at the audition mate?"

"Great. They hired me on the spot. They're still looking for a lead guitarist so as soon as they find one the other two guitarists will quit as they're starting up another band on their own. Don't you play trumpet Richard?"

"I've been paying since I was seven. I also play the guitar but I don't have one at the moment."

"Why don't you try out for the band with ya trumpet and ya can use my guitar for the audition? If they like what you do ya could always buy a guitar and amp and you'd be making money."

"How do I get in touch with them?"

"I know the bass player, Brad. He's a good bloke. I played with him in a band once before."

"That sounds fucking great Clint! I need more money and something to cheer me up. My life is total shit at the moment."

"Drink up Richard, I'll go grab us a couple of pints and while I'm there I'll give Brad a ring. Ya never know."

While I sat there waiting for Clint to come back, I started to think what it would be like to play in a band and make money out of it. That would be a great way to make some extra money now that Jonna has quit her job and refuses to work. It would balance out my shitty life with her until I can deliver the bitch back to her mother in Denmark.

It didn't take long before Clint came back to the table with two pints in his hands and a smile on his face.

"How did ya go mate?" I asked.

"Yeah, good Richard. He's really interested. He asked if you can go for an audition tomorrow night as they're anxious to get rid of the other two blokes who've lost interest and it's causing tension in the band."

"Yeah, no worries Clint, as long as I can use your guitar and amp."

"No problem there Richard. I'll go with you and introduce ya. We won't need the amp 'cause they've got two amps there that belong to the other blokes. Ya can use one of them. We've got to be there at 8 o'clock. It's in Halifax so we can meet here at seven and catch a double-decker. That way, we'll be there in plenty of time."

"That sounds fantastic Clint. It's just what I need at this time in mi life."

"Me too mate. That missus of mine is driving me fucking nuts and as far as shaggin' goes, it's been so long now since I've seen her pussy, it's probably healed up."

"I know what ya mean, Jonna's the same way. I've had more wanks since I've been with her than the whole of mi life in the Outback as a single bloke!"

After a couple more pints with Clint, we parted company with the intention of meeting up the following evening. On the way home, I decided not

113

to say anything about auditioning for a gig in a cabaret band until I was sure I'd got the job.

When I got home, she was in a stinking mood 'cause I'd been in the pub with Clint for a couple of hours. I decided to keep my mouth shut. Instead of buying into her new drama, I gave Anthony a bath and got him ready for bed. Before going to bed myself, I put mi trumpet outside in the garage so I could take it with me to the audition without her knowing. That evening, as I lay in bed next to her, I never said a word as I knew once I started talking to her about refusing to work, the shit would hit the fan. Besides, my mind was really happy at the prospect of playing music and touring the Working Men's clubs in an established cabaret band.

I'd already decided that if I got the job, I'd buy a guitar and amp on time-payment. Even though I didn't like buying anything that way as up to now in my life, I had always paid cash for small purchases. It was the way my mother brought me up. "Don't ever get in debt Richard, 'cause whoever you're in debt to owns you until you've paid it off." she'd say. With the exception of the mortgage for the house, I have stuck to that advice my mother taught me all those years ago.
The following evening, as I was getting dressed up to go out, Jonna was still in her shitty mood about my intention to sell the house. We had barely spoken two words to each other since I'd been home from work.
"Why you putting on good clothes Richard? Where you go?"

"I'm going for an interview for a part-time job."

"Why you do that? You already have job."

"I've told ya already, we can't keep this house on one wage. Seeing as you refuse to get another job then I'm gonna get one."

"What new job you get?"

"I'll let you know if I get it."

"Why you no tell me now?"

"'Cause I don't want to alright. I'll probably be home around 10-ish."

"Fuck you Richard! Me no care if you don't come home. Why you not find another woman to live with, then you get as much sex as you want?"

"Very funny Jonna. Where do you think you and Anthony are gonna' live if I do that?"

"I go back Denmark with Anthony. My mother let me live at her house."

"Where's the money coming from for the fares? Do you have it? I certainly don't!"

"Me have no money. I give you for rent."

"Right. That was the deal when we bought this new house."

I found Clint in the pub, finishing off the last few drops of a pint.

"Clint, how are ya mate? Are ya ready to go?"

"I sure am Richard. I was just wetting mi whistle while I was waiting for ya."

"Am I late?"

"No mate, I walked over early just to get out of the house. The missus is winging and moaning again."

"What about?"

"Oh, same old shit. I'm not doing enough work, not making enough money and drinking too much beer."

"Sounds like she's covered all the bases mate."

"Yeah, the only thing she didn't complain about was not gettin' enough sex." We both had a good laugh about that joke as we picked up our instruments and took off to the bus stop to catch the double-decker to Halifax.

When we got to the room where the audition was to take place, there was no one around so we found the closest pub where it was warm and cosy and ordered a couple of pints. We hadn't been there very long before Brad, the bass guitarist, walked in with his bass.

"Clint, how are ya?" he said as he put his bass down next to our instruments. "I'll just grab a quick pint before we go. I had a stinking fucking day at college. I need a liquid relaxant."

Once Brad was sat down at the table with his pint, he said, "My names Brad." and offered his hand.

"Richard." I said and shook hands with him.

"Clint tells me you play a mean trumpet."

"Yeah that's right. I also play guitar pretty good, although the trumpet is mi first instrument."

"Well that's great. Having a trumpet in the band would certainly give us a lot more variety."

Brad was a tall, lanky bloke with a well-trimmed beard and a full head of hair which came down to just below his ear lobes. He was about 32 years old. He had decided to go back to college to get another degree which would give him access to a better paying job. He seemed like an easy bloke to get on with so we hit it off right from the start. Once our pints were gone he said, "Ya think we should head over to the rehearsal room? The others will probably be there by now."

When we arrived at the practice room, the drummer, whose name was Roy, was just tuning up his drum kit and Dawn and her husband were testing out the PA system. Roy owned a pretty new Transit Van that he transported the band's gear around in. He was a medium built bloke and was very friendly.

Clint introduced me to Dawn and her husband who wished me well on the audition. After I had a quick look at their repertoire, we picked out 3 middle-of-the-road songs and ran through them.
"What about the trumpet Richard? I'm anxious to hear what we can do with that as a band. It would give us an edge on the other groups that tour the circuits." said Brad. I suggested a couple of Herb Alpert numbers that Brad had played in another band when he toured Europe. After writing out a chord chart for Clint, who was not so familiar with the songs, we ran through them much to the delight of Brad, who had a big smile on his face. Clint fucked up a couple of chord changes but all in all, everything sounded good, to say it was the first time we had played together.
"Do you have your own guitar and amp Richard?" asked Dawn.
"Not yet love. It depends on whether I get the job or not."
"Tell ya what Richard," said Brad. "Why don't you wait for us across the road at the pub and we'll be over there in a while. We need to make a decision, as a band, if this is a direction we want to go in."

Sitting in the pub, sipping on a pint, I was quite anxious as I waited for the verdict. By this time, I had gotten used to the idea of playing music and making money out of it. I didn't have long to wait before Brad, Clint and Roy showed up at the pub. Clint gave me a little wink as he walked towards the table.

As soon as they were sat down Brad said, "Well we discussed a few ideas and then took a vote. It's unanimous, you are officially a paid member of Dawn and the Daybreakers! We do a five-way split with the money and we all contribute to the petrol money for Roy's transit van, which we'd be fucked without."

Clint said, "Congratulations Richard, I knew you'd pass the audition. I'm buying the first round. What are you gonna' have Roy?"

"Get me an orange juice Clint."

"How can ya drink that putrid shit." said Clint, jokingly. "Why don't you have a beer?"

"No mate, I'm driving. The last thing I need is to get stopped and lose mi license. I haven't finished paying off the Tranny Van yet and I need it for work. I'd be fucked without mi license."

When I got home that evening, Jonna was asleep on the couch with the TV going and Anthony was in his bed.

"Where you been Richard, it's 10 o'clock?"

"I told you I'd be home around 10."

"You get another work?"

"Yeah, I auditioned for a cabaret band called Dawn and the Daybreakers. I got the job playing trumpet and guitar."

"You play in fucking band now?"

"Yeah, four night a week, sometimes 5."

"So, you never fucking home anymore. Why you not get other work?"

"Because I want to play music professionally now."

"I no want you play in band. There will be girls after you."

"I didn't join the band for that reason; besides, you refuse to work so where is the money going to come from to keep us with the bills?"

"I no care about bills. You stay home with me and Anthony.""

"Can't do that anymore Jonna. We need extra money and I've already accepted the job."

"You only get music man job so you can have other woman."

"That's not true. Even if it was, aren't you the one who's always telling me to go find another woman for sex if I want it?"

"Fuck you Richard. You no get more sex from me."

"You know what Jonna, fuck you too! I'm off to bed. I've got to be up early for work. Are you coming or not?"

"No, I sleep on couch tonight. I no sleep with you."

"Please ya fucking self, see if I care. I slept on mi own for years before I met you so it's no great loss."

"Fuck you Bastard." she said as I left the room and walked up the stairs.

Anthony had his own small bedroom now, so before going to bed, I stuck mi head around the door of his room to make sure all was well with him. Then I hit the sack. The next day, I finished work a couple of hours early and caught a train into Manchester with the intent of buying miself a guitar and amp. I didn't have enough money to buy the gear for cash but the bloke who ran the second-hand music store was a decent bloke. He agreed to do the deal on hire-purchase for me. I put a small deposit down knowing I'd still have enough money to pay the mortgage. I would now be making extra money playing in the band. After playing a few guitars, I settled on a white Fender 69 Telecaster and a Vox A.C.30 that had a treble booster built in the back panel. Sitting on the train on my way home, I was contemplating how life was slowly changing for me. I had a good day job as was now able to make some extra money playing music in the clubs, which I was really looking forward to. Another great benefit would be, I'll be able to practice new songs at home which would fill in the time when Jonna had the shits and wouldn't speak to me for hours on end. There was one small problem that I hadn't anticipated. His name was Anthony! Every time I got the guitar out to play, he would walk over to my chair and try to pluck the strings with his hand, right in the middle of a song that I was practicing. At first, I held the guitar for him and let him plunk on the strings thinking that he's soon get fed up with it. That was not to be the case.

The next time I went into Halifax to do the weeks shopping, I went into a toy shop and bought a cheap plastic guitar for him, thinking that he'd have fun playing his own guitar. Not so! He played around with it for a few minutes and then threw it on the floor and said, "Anthony's guitar no good. Daddy's guitar!"

The plastic guitar didn't last for more than 24 hours before the gut strings were broken off and the back of it had a big hole in it from kicking it around the room like a football! The only other option left for me was to practice in the bedroom, with a chair behind the door handle so he couldn't get in and disturb my playing.

A couple of days later, I had another incident to deal with. I went upstairs to practice a new song for the band. When I opened the guitar case, I found, to my horror, all the strings had been cut in two with a pair of scissors. When I walked into the living room, I said to Jonna, "You fucking mean-spirited crazy bitch! You just couldn't stand me getting a little bit of happiness out of mi music could you? You had to cut all the strings off mi Telecaster didn't ya!"
"Fuck you Richard, why you should be happy? Me no happy you go out at night and play in band."

The first thing that came up in my mind was to go back upstairs and take off what was left of the E string and garrote the fucking bitch with it. I was now at my wits end with her insanity!
"One day, Jonna, you'll go too fucking far and I'll knock ya arse over head, ya crazy bitch."
"You touch me, I call police and you go jail. Me and Anthony have good life here without you!"
"And who do you think is going to pay the mortgage, ya gormless git?"
Lucky for me, the guitar case came with a set of keys. From that moment on, I never put the Telecaster back in the case without locking it.

121

19

MI DAD COMES TO VISIT
~A DISASTER ~

One Friday afternoon, I was shopping at Sowerby
Bridge Open-air market. I was very familiar with
this market as I had been shopping there with mi
mother since we moved to Boston Street, after she
left mi dad for Jim Bailey. My job was to lump the
bags around for her as she searched the stalls for the
day's bargains.

I was just about finished my shopping when I ran
into mi dad who was buying pigs heads and trotters
for the soup he would make for himself, now that he
lived alone.

"How are ya dad?" I asked.

"Not too bad lad. How are you?"

"I'm alright dad. I'd be a lot better if it wasn't for this
cold weather."

"You're cold at your age? Wait till ya my age lad and
you'll know what cold is. My bloody lumbago's
playing up something bloody awful. I can hardly get
out a' bed in the mornings and when I do, I'm stuck
in front of mi coal fire all day."

"Have ya finished shopping yet dad?"

"Just about. I need a cabbage for mi soup, then I'm
done."

"D'ya wanna' go for a pint when ya done?"

"Aye, that sounds alright to me lad. In fact, it's the
best bloody idea I've heard all day. At least we'll be
inside where it's warm."

 Once we found a comfortable place to sit, I said,

122

"My shout dad. What d'ya want?"

"A pint of bitter will be alright lad. They serve a good drop in here."

Once we had our beers, we chatted about life in general. It didn't take long for mi dad to bring up the subject of mi mother.

"How's that ex-wench of mine doing?"

"Ya mean mi mother?"

"Aye, who bloody else would I mean."

"I don't know dad. I haven't seen her for ages. She moved out of Boston Street and lives in Cleethorpes now."

"Bloody good job. That means I won't have to run into her at the market. Is she still living with that fat poofta Jim Bailey?"

"As far as I know, she is."

"I'll bet she's leading that fat faggot on a right song and dance, same as she tried to do to me."

"She seemed pretty happy with him the last time I saw her."

"That bloody wench will never be happy as long as her arsehole points to the ground. She was put on this earth to make any man's life she's involved with a bloody misery. How are you gettin' on with that bloody foreign wench ya took up with."

"Not too good dad. She's a bit of a nutter most of the time. Sometimes she's alright though but it doesn't last for long."

"They're all the same those bloody wench's lad. We're a damn sight better off without 'em. If they're not nagging a man to death about something or the other, they're rubbing that bloody minge of theirs up and down a man's leg of a night-time 'cause they

123

want something. I'm telling ya lad, if they didn't have a minge, they wouldn't have a bloody friend in the world."

"Well maybe they're not all the same dad."

"Don't you bloody well fool ya self. Take a tip from ya old dad and stay away from the buggers. You'd be better off in the long run." Mi dad's pint was almost empty so I said to him, "Finish up ya pint dad and I'll get ya another before we go."

"It's my turn lad. You bought the first ones."

"It's alright dad, I'll get 'em. Besides, you're on a pension and I'm working."

Once we had started our second pint, my dad started on another of his pet peeves.

"Talking about pensions lad, you know what that bloody Labor government just did? They gave me a 5 and sixpence raise and then the bloody council raised mi rent by 4 shillings and seven pence and the Electric company raised their rates and now I'm one and 6 pence worse off! What this bloody country needs is a good, old-fashioned revolution! We need to drag the buggers out of that Parliament of ours and string the thieving sods up to lamp-posts and leave 'em there. That would make the next ones think twice before trying to rob us all blind. I don't like those French bloody frogs but they had the right idea lad, with that guillotine. They chopped off their bloody heads. That stopped their shenanigans for a few years! To think I fought in the bloody trenches of World War 1 to live in a rotten and corrupt country like this. A man needs his bloody head testing."

"Well maybe when the other party gets into power it

will improve dad."

"Have you lost ya bloody marbles lad? Those bleeding conservatives are worse. All they ever do is give their rich, bum-boy Earls and Dukes another inheritance tax cut and take it out of the working mans' pay packet. It's bloody disgusting! They're all a bunch a' bloody shirt-lifters. This bloody country of ours has gone to dogs. There's no bloody hope left for the working man anymore."

Mi dad tipped up the last remains of his pint and looked up at the clock on the wall,

"Jesus Christ Almighty lad, is that the bloody time?"

"Yeah, it's nearly closing time dad. D'ya want another before ya go?"

"Not for me lad. I've got to get home and cook up mi pigs head and trotters for mi dinner tonight, otherwise, I'll be eating bread and lard again! Ya never know lad, I might win the pools tonight and if that's the case I'll be living high on the hog."

"Hey dad, why don't ya come to my place for Sunday dinner?"

"Are ya still living in that cottage up Sowerby New Road?"

"No, I sold it and bought a real good semi-detached place, halfway up Pye Nest Road. Ya know where that is?"

"Aye, on the way to Halifax."

"Yeah right. ya could ask the bus conductor to tell ya when 52 comes up. The bust stops right outside my place. Ya could see ya grandson Anthony. He's grown quite a bit since ya last saw him in his pram at the market."

"Is that bloody foreign wench of yours gonna' be there."

"Yeah, we're gonna' have a roast, that's if she doesn't have the shits and if she does, I'll cook it up."

"I'm not sure that's a good idea lad. Last time I spoke to that bloody wench at the market, I couldn't understand a word she said."

"She speaks a lot better English now. She probably won't speak much anyway."

"That'll suit me down to the bloody ground. She ought to go back to school to learn to speak good English. They're all the same, these bloody wogs. They come over here to live in our country and make damn good money and to add insult to injury, they can't be bothered to learn the language!"

"So, will ya come or not? I'll get a few Newcastle Browns in. They'll go good with a roast and baked potatoes."

"Aye, alright then I suppose I'll come. What time d'ya want me there?"

"Around 2 o'clock. Does that sound alright?"

"Aye, I'll get the 1 o'clock bus from my place." With that said, I walked mi dad to his bus stop and waited with him till his bus came.

"I'll see ya on Sunday at 2." I said as he got on the bus.

"Aye, I suppose so lad." He walked inside the bus and took off back to his council house at 36 Jubilee Terrace near Ripponden.

When Sunday afternoon rolled around, I stood outside, at the bus stop, waiting for mi dad's double-decker to arrive from Ripponden.

"How are ya dad?" I said as he got off the bus in his good suit and top coat.

Mi dad was one of the best-dressed men I'd ever seen. As well as his double-breasted dark gray suit

126

and navy blue top coat, he always wore a well-creased Trilby hat on a jaunty angle.

"I'm alright lad. I asked the bus conductor to tell me when we got to your stop but the bugger went and forgot, so it's just as well you were waiting for me. I might have ended up in Kings bloody Cross!"

"Oh well, ya here now dad. Let's get inside before I freeze mi bloody nuts off. If ya don't mind, don't forget to wipe ya feet good 'cause Jonna's a bit of a neurotic as far as keeping the front room neat and tidy."

"Ya think I'm bloody stupid lad? I've lived with women before ya know. They're a pain in the bloody arse at the best of times."

Once mi dad's coat and hat were hung up in the entrance way, we walked into the Lounge room. Jonna was in the kitchen finishing off the Sunday roast that she agreed to cook but not until I agreed to take her clothes shopping to Halifax. Black-mailing bitch! Anthony, who was playing with his toys on the floor, was quite surprised to see a stranger in our front room and ran into the kitchen to tell his mother.

"Here dad, sit over here in my chair, next to the fire. It'll keep ya warm."

"Aye alright, but ya can turn that bloody fire down? This room's like a bloody oven already."

"Yeah, we've got central heating in every room."

"That must cost ya a bloody fortune to run lad?"

"It's not cheap but they reckon it's less expensive to keep it on instead of turning it on and off, 'cause it takes a while for the radiators to warm up again."

After mi dad was comfortable, I went into the kitchen to get a couple bottles of Newcastle Brown.
"Mi dad's here Jonna."
"Me know, Anthony told me."
"Are ya coming out to say Hello?"
"Am busy making dinner. Take Anthony out of the kitchen before he causes a problem."
"Come on Anthony. Let's go and meet ya Grandad."
"Me carry." he said, once he saw the beer bottles."
"No mate, you'll end up dropping them."
"Anthony no drop." he said as he tried to reach up and grab a bottle.
"Alright, here ya go. Be careful. Ya know what ya mother's like with the carpet." Wonder of wonders, he made it to the chair where mi dad was sitting and said, "Beer."
"Good lad." said mi dad as he took the bottle from Anthony's hand. I handed mi dad his glass for the beer and he poured a generous amount into it and said, "Cheers lad!"
"Cheers Dad." After he'd had a mouth full, I said, "The beers all right for ya?"
"Aye but it's a bit bloody cold."
"Yeah, it's been in the fridge. Give it a minute and it'll warm up."
Once he'd put his beer down on the hearth, he said to Anthony, "Ya wanna' sit on ya Grandads knee?" Anthony was a bit shy at first as he hadn't seen his grandad for quite a while. That didn't last long and the next minute he was climbing all over mi dads lap. First thing he did, he made a grab for mi dad's eyeglasses as he'd never seen a pair up close before. Mi dad managed to get his glasses back and said, "Here, ya can play with the case. Ya

128

can't do much damage to that." Little did mi dad
know what Anthony was like til he saw him trying
to pull the lining out of it.

"Better give me that case lad. I don't want it
knackered. I haven't had it long." said mi dad to
Anthony.

Anthony, reluctantly gave mi dad his spectacle case
back and then said, "Anthony drink."

"What does he want?" asked mi dad.

"He wants a sip of ya beer." I said.

"Alright lad, here ya go, but I can tell ya before ya
start, ya won't like it!" Anthony took a big gulp out
of mi dad's glass. As soon as he swallowed it, he
coughed at the same time and blurted out the beer all
over mi dad's good suit and over the arm of the
armchair.

"Ah shit!" I said. "Come on Anthony, hop off
Grandads knee so he can drink his beer in peace."

"I'll get ya a wet cloth before the beer dries out."

Back in the kitchen, I said to Jonna, "Give us a
damp cloth will ya? Anthony has spilled some beer
on mid dad's good suit and on the armchair."

"Why you give your dad beer in my good room?
You make him sit in dining room!"

"He's not sitting in the dining room. He's alright
where he is. Anyway, it was Anthony's fault, not mi
dads. He wanted a drink of mi dad's beer."

"He give my son beer now?"

"No, don't be bloody silly lass. He just gave him a
little sip."

I took the damp cloth back to mi dad so he could
sponge off his suit. The next minute, Jonna walked
into the room with another cloth. "What's that cloth

for?" I asked.

"What about my good chair? Where did the beer spill?"

"It didn't spill. A bit of spray went on it when Anthony spit it out." Mi dad put his beer in the hearth again and moved his arm so Jonna could wipe off the arm of the chair.

"Aren't ya gonna' say hello to mi dad Jonna?"

"Hello." she said, then went back to the kitchen. She was back in the room in a flash with a cork beer mat which she placed under mi dad's glass. As soon as he bent over in the chair to pick up his beer before Anthony could get his hands on it, she pulled the good cushion and placed it neatly on the couch. Anthony tried to climb back up on mi dad's knee but he wasn't having a bar of it. He picked him up and sat him on the floor.

Mi dad was 70 years old. He didn't have much patience with kids and it was obvious he didn't want Anthony climbing all over him, trying to get into his pockets and grab his glass case again.

"Come on Anthony, let's get your toy box out. Ya can play in the dining room."

"Don't bother on my account lad. I'm going home."

"But you haven't had dinner yet. Why are you going?"

"A man knows when he's not bloody welcome lad. That friggin' wench of yours doesn't want me in the house in case I mess up her bloody showroom. Not to mention the dirty look she gave me when she brought the beer coaster in and then flogged the bloody pillow from mi chair!"

"Don't go yet dad. She doesn't mean it. Stay and

have some dinner."

"Not bloody likely! That foreign cow's as bad as ya bloody mother was. She might even be a bit worse if that's at all bloody possible. How come ya ended up with a bloody thing like that? All I can say is she must be a bloody good ride to put up with her nonsense!" There was no talking mi dad out of leaving as he put on his hat, coat and muffler. That was the last time he ever visited me.

20

A PARTY TO END ALL PARTIES

A month after the incident with inviting mi dad for dinner, I asked the members of the band if they'd like to come for a party at my place, on one of the rare Friday nights we had off.

"What's your missus gonna say about that?" asked Clint who was well aware of Jonna's neurosis about keeping the front room like a 5-star showroom.

"I haven't told her yet but don't worry about that mate. I'll take care of it."

"Oh, by the way Jonna," I said one evening when she appeared to be in a somewhat good mood.

"We're having a bit of a party next Friday night. I invited the blokes from the band and their wives for a few drinks."

"What you say Richard? We not having party at my place! They'll make a mess! They'll spill beer all over the place and end up burning my new carpet!"

"No they won't. They're good people and they will be careful."

"No Richard, I not having anyone partying here."

"Well, you know what Jonna? It's too late now 'cause I've already invited them and furthermore where did you get the idea from that this is your house? It belongs to all three of us."

"No, this my house!"

"So you're going to pay the mortgage at the end of the month are ya?"

"Me have no money."

"There's a good reason you have no money and that's because you refuse to work."

"Me no like work in this country. Me like work in Denmark."

"Yeah, well we're not in Denmark, are we? So, we're having a party whether you like it or not!"

For the next three days she never spoke to me except for the bare minimum. She also employed one of her blackmail tactics which was to load herself up on Hed-X tablets and sit in the chair in her nightdress, staring out the window. She also would not do anything for Anthony while I was in the house. It was left up to me to make him something to eat, change his clothes when needed and get him ready for bed. On many occasions before, I had given in to her blackmail just to keep a bit of peace in the house but this time I'd had enough. I was determined the party would go ahead as planned.

I have heard tell, in my travels, that every man marries a version of his mother and that every woman marries a version of her father. While I cannot prove that as a fact, what I can say is that Jonna definitely had one of mi mother's traits as far as not speaking to me. In days gone by, as a boy, anytime I messed up, according to mi mother's rules, she would say to me, "That's it lad, I'm not speaking to you anymore." and she meant it! No matter how much I tried to get her to speak to me, I failed at every turn. It took a while for me to figure out how to get around mi mother's little habit. In the end I did it. After three days of not speaking to me, she started to relent by saying a few odd words. What did I do? I refused to answer her for a couple of days. Let me tell you, did that get her goat. So

133

much so that she would eventually take the bamboo curtain rod out of the window and give me a bloody good hiding with it. Getting the backs of one's bare legs belted with a bamboo cane hurts like you can't imagine, unless you've experienced it yourself. It took a few years for me to cure mi mother of playing her game. In the end, I won that battle.

Friday night was now upon us. I had informed my guests that it was a BYO party as I was not rolling in money, which they totally understood as they were all in the same position. I bought a couple of bottles of inexpensive wine and half a dozen bottles of beer. I also bought a good quality plastic tablecloth and covered the dining room table with it as I, myself, didn't want to get anything burned. Clint and his wife were the first to arrive. When I opened the door and greeted them, Clint's old lady said, "I hope you don't mind, we had to bring our daughter along as our babysitter let us down at the last minute."
"No worries, love. She can play with Anthony. He's not going to want to go to bed with a party going on in the house." Roy and his wife, Brad and his missus and half an hour later, a couple of friends and their wives from the pub across the street showed up. The French doors between the lounge and the dining room had been opened to make more room for my guests to freely walk around. We were all set for a big party!

When I say, 'big party' I don't mean a big piss-up that ends in a brawl at the end of the night. It was more like a friendly get-together with wine, beer, peanuts and crisps. One of the wives brought some sausage rolls and pork pies. Another wife brought a large plate of ham and cheese sandwiches. We had plenty of everything.

"Where's Jonna?" asked Roy's wife.

"She's got the shits. She's upstairs in the bedroom. She says she's not coming down."

"Oh, that's not good." said Susan. "Would you like me to go upstairs and have a chat with her?"

"Help ya self love. She won't come down 'cause she thinks we're gonna mess up the house."

"Well there's no way that's going to happen as everyone can see, you've got a beautiful home."

Ten minutes later, Susan came back downstairs and said, "Jonna's getting changed. She'll be down in a bit."

"Ya kidding? Ya talked her into it?"

"Yeah, it took a while but I assured her that no one would disrespect her house."

Half an hour later, Jonna made her grand entrance. She had applied her makeup, done her hair and put on her best dress. All of the wives were happy see that she was attending the party. They stood around talking to her. Some of them made sure she had a glass of wine, a smoke and something to eat. It was a great little get-together. Halfway through the night Jonna was having as good a time as anyone else. That was due to the amount of wine she was drinking. It made my heart really happy to see her enjoying herself for a change. She even started to talk to me and at one point she put her arm around me which almost sobered me up, from the shock. Anthony and Clint's young daughter were having fun jumping up and down on the couch when no one was sat on it, which didn't seem to faze Jonna at all. By this time, she was getting quite drunk. It was getting late and Jonna was drunk. So much so that she had to sit down before she fell down. At one point she put her glass of wine on the carpet next to her chair and without realizing it, she knocked it over. If that wasn't enough, she put her cigarette in the ashtray and forgot about it. As it slowly burned away, it became unbalanced and fell out of the ashtray. Brad, who was about the only non-smoker saw what had happened and said to Jonna. "Hey Jonna, ya spilled wine, love and ya cigarette has fallen out of the ashtray." Jonna, who was moving very slowly by now, had trouble moving forward in the chair to pick up the lit cigarette and was in no state to go to the kitchen for a cloth to clean up the spilled red wine. Brad said to her, "It's alright Jonna, I'll get it for you."

Brad bent down to pick up the cigarette but not before it had burned a hole in the new carpet. "I'm afraid you've burned a hole in the carpet Jonna. I'll go get ya a dishcloth so ya can mop up the wine before it stains."

What came out of Jonna's mouth was the second surprise of the night, "Fuck carpet! Who cares! It's a party. Let's have fun. A bit of wine and burn isn't going to hurt anybody!" Seeing what was happening, I took off into the kitchen for a cloth with a bit of dish liquid on it and then proceeded to wipe up the spilled wine and inspect the hole in the carpet.

"Why you worry Richard, is only a bit of wine."

"Yeah, but you burned a small hole in the carpet Jonna."

"Who care! I having fun!"

After that, all I could say was, "D'ya want some more wine?"

"Yeah, me want more wine and cigarettes."

The time was getting on. It was close to midnight. One at a time, the guests started to leave but not before the wives helped me to clean up the empty bottles and wash up the plates that had been used for the food.

"Why everybody leaving?" said Jonna, in her drunken state. "It's a party!"

"It's 12 o'clock." said Clint's wife. "We should be getting home."

"No, me like party all night. More wine!"

"I think ya might have had enough. Besides Anthony has fallen asleep on the couch." I said. Once everybody had left, I cleaned up the few odd items that were left and then picked up Anthony and put him to bed. I helped Jonna upstairs to bed in case she fell and hurt herself. Once she saw the bed, she fell straight forward, face first onto it.

"Don't ya wanna' take off ya good dress Jonna?"

"No, you take off Richard and I give you 'fucky, fucky'!"

By the time I had taken her dress off and hung it up in her side of the wardrobe, she was dead to the world. I straightened her up, covered her with the quilt. That's where she stayed till lunch time the next day.

21

DRUNK ON THE MOORS
~ MUTTON FOR SUNDAY DINNER ~

Playing with Dawn and the Daybreakers was still going well as we were doing four gigs a week which meant that after I had paid the weekly payments on the gear, I was still left with a few quid which went towards the mortgage and the bills which on some months could be quite high depending on how cold the weather was. One Saturday night, we were playing at a Working Men's Club in Rochdale. The audience was in fine spirits and loved the middle of the road type music we played for them. Our first spot usually lasted for about twenty minutes. As soon as it was over, we would take a break for half-an-hour to decide which songs we would play for our second spot.

The band always had a reserved table to relax at. At these times, one of us would buy a round of pints. Dawn, who was not much of a drinker would never buy a round as she would only ever drink a Shandy, which was a mix of lemonade and beer. Brad, Clint and myself loved having a few pints at the gigs as it was a night out and we were making money. Roy, the drummer, who was a real good bloke, very seldom drank more than two half-pints the whole evening as he was responsible for getting us to the gig on time in his Transit Van and making sure we arrived home safe. I have no idea why but Roy, who was usually quiet, was in a good mood this evening. I said to him, "It's my round Roy, half-pint as

138

usual?"

"Nah Richard, I think I'll break out and have a pint tonight."

"Jesus Roy, what's going on mate? Ya usually only have a half. Did you get a shag off the missus before ya left home?"

"I wish Richard. No, I just feel like having a few beers tonight."

"No worries Mate, one pint coming up." The fact that Roy was having a pint, rather than his usual half-pint, didn't go un-noticed by the rest of the band. Brad, our bass player said to me when Roy wasn't around, "So what's with Roy? He's had about three pints tonight so far. Is he celebrating or something?"

"I don't know Brad. I asked him if he got a shag before he left home but he said no, he just felt like a few beers."

As the evening wore on, Roy kept up with the three of us, beer for beer. By the end of the evening he was firing on all 8 cylinders.

"Are you alright to drive Roy?" said Dawn as we packed the last of the gear into the back of his van.

"Yeah, no problem. I do drink when I'm not doing a gig you know."

"I wasn't criticizing ya Roy. It's just that ya don't usually drink so much at gigs"

"Don't worry Dawn, I won't run us off the road. I've got a lot of money invested in the van and mi drum kit which I still haven't finished pay for yet."

Our usual habit was to buy half a dozen bottles before closing time so we could have a beer on the

139

way home. Roy, who was Mr. Responsibility was driving. No worries there. As we drove away from the club and got down the road heading off from Rochdale, Roy piped and said, "Ya got a spare bottle back there?"

"Yeah, sure." said Clint and passed an open bottle to him from the back seat, where we usually sat. Brad, who was the oldest, raised one of his eyebrows as Roy took a quick drink from his bottle and then stuck it between his legs. Dawn, who always sat next to Roy, had a worried look on her face every time Roy took a drink from his bottle.

Once we got through Littleborough and the houses started to thin out a bit, Roy drained the last of his beer, wound down the window and then hurled the bottle over the roof of the Transit Van onto a stretch of land that was empty. Winding the window up without missing a beat, he said to Clint, "Open another bottle for me. That's the best tasting beer I've had for a while."

Clint, who was in charge of opening the bottles, passed the beer to Dawn who then handed it to Roy who had consumed quite a lot of beer by now, never strayed an inch from the center of our side of the road. If one didn't know, they'd swear he was sober.

By this time, we were at the bottom of Blackstone Hedge and were looking at a long climb to the top of the Moors. Once we were at the top, there were mobs of Black-Face sheep sitting on the side of the road. Some were wandering up and down looking for a feed.

"You will be careful of the sheep?" said Dawn as

one ran across the road in front of us. Suddenly, I piped up and said, "No worries Roy, if ya hit one we can put it in the back with the gear and when we get back to my place I'll butcher it, then skin it and cut it up. It'll make a good feed."

"Hey, that's not a bad idea Richard." said Roy. "I could do with some free mutton. I've got four kids to feed."

"Are you serious Roy?"

"Course I am."

"Then get off the main road and we'll chase one down with the van. As soon as it tires out, I'll hang out the side door and jump on it."

"Are you sure ya know how to butcher it Richard? I don't want to drive the van over these rough Moors for nothing."

"Course I do Roy. I learned how to do it in the Outback of Australia. I'm not just a pretty face ya know!"

"You're not serious, are you?" said Dawn, who was now looking quite panic stricken.

"Why not Dawn?" I said. "Mutton's really expensive. It's not something I can afford every week."

Once Brad realized that Roy was not joking, he said, "Fun's fun Roy, but it might be better if we just drive straight home."

"Nah, fuck it!" said Roy who didn't usually swear. "Let's just do it!"

"Let's put it to a vote then." said Brad. "All those in favor of driving straight home, raise ya hand." Brad and Dawn were the only ones to raise their hands. Clint said, "Well, I guess that settles it. It looks like we're having roast Mutton for Sunday dinner."

"So how do we go about this Richard?" said Roy, as he slowed down the van.

"As soon as I see a youngish one Roy, I'll point it out to ya and we'll chase it down and separate it from the rest of the mob."

"I can't believe you're going to do this Roy." said Dawn, who was now hanging on to her seat belt with both hands.

"Ya see that one there Roy, drive on that side of it. It'll run out that way." I said. Roy pulled the van off the main road and headed out over the rough Moors. The Black-Face sheep started to run a bit as it realized the Tranny Van was following it. "Change place with me Clint so I can jump out of the side door when we get close enough." I said.

The Black Face was now running faster in the head-lights. I said to Roy, "Go faster mate, we're not keeping up with it!"

"I'm not so sure this is a good idea Richard. I didn't realize sheep could run this fast! Besides that, these Moors have got pot holes and stones all over them."

"Don't worry about it Roy, just drive faster. He'll soon tire out."

Roy stepped on the accelerator and the van was starting to bounce all over the place. The amps and gear in the back of the van were starting to bounce around as we sped across the Moors. Clint, who was pretty drunk said, "This is fucking great! It's the most fun I've had since I was a single man!"

Dawn was still hanging onto her seat belt. She was too scared to say a word. By this time, Brad, who was quite a conservative bloke was hanging onto the back of Dawn's seat as he bounced up and down on

142

his seat. At one time, he hit his head on the roof of the van.

"He's tiring out Roy! Try and get alongside of him." I yelled out.

As Roy moved closer to him, the sheep made a sudden turn and headed in another direction. "Spin around Roy!" I yelled. "We've almost got him now!" Roy turned the steering wheel and all the amps slid to the side and made a loud banging sound.

"We're going to wreck the gear!" said Brad. "This is bloody stupid. I've had that amp of mine for 15 years."

"Don't worry about it Brad, we've nearly got him."

The Black Face was now slowing down, so I said to Roy, "Pull alongside of him Roy. Get as close as ya can!"

The side door of the van was now open as I clung to the door. The sheep was about two feet away from the side door by now. I decided, it's now or never! "Yee Haw!" I said and leapt out of the door. I landed on the back end of the sheep. Due to being so drunk and the strength of the Black-Face, he escaped my grip. Picking myself up as fast as I could, I took off after him in hot pursuit.

I would never have caught him had it not been for Roy, who assessed the situation and drove up fast behind him and then bumped his rear-end with the front bumper of the van which knocked the sheep over like a pin in a bowling alley. Wasting no time, I jumped on him and rolled him over on his back. Roy turned the van around and shone the headlights on myself and the sheep as I sat him up on his arse.

Although we'd run him to ground for about 10 minutes, he still had plenty of fight left in him and was raring to go!

Roy put the van in neutral and got out from behind the steering wheel to inspect the van for damage.

"Good as gold Richard. Not a mark on it. A bit of wool on the bumper bar, that's it."

"Now what?" said Clint as he jumped out of the van, still drunk.

"Now we tie him up and make room for him in the back of the van. Hey Roy, you got any rope in the van mate?" I said.

"Sure have. I always keep some for emergencies and this looks like one of those times."

Once Roy had found the rope and a knife to cut it with, Brad, who was now out of the van said, "I don't fucking believe this. I've never seen anything like it in mi life and I've done a lot of traveling in mi days."

"Ah, this is nothing Brad. We do things like this in the Bush every day."

"In that case, I think I'll stay in England. It sounds safer."

"How ya gonna tie it up?" asked Clint who was standing over the sheep due to the fact he'd never seen one up close before.

"I'll show ya mate. There's a special way of doing it."

"Look at the horns on him!" said Roy who was now inspecting his Sunday dinner.

"I'll bet they'd hurt if he stabbed ya with them." said Brad.

Once the Black-Face was in the van and the initial

144

euphoria and joking had died down, I had a few moments of inner reflection. 'What the fuck was I thinking? Chasing a full grown sheep across the Moors in mi trendy platform boots, bell bottom trousers, frilly shirt and long hair which fell below mi shoulders and to cap it all off, I still had sparkly glitter under mi eyes from our last spot of the evening when we cranked up the volume and played rock songs that the audience could dance to. Had anyone, except the band members, seen me they would have thought I'd escaped from a lunatic asylum! For a split moment, I was having a few doubts mi self about my mental stability!'

It didn't take us long to get home from our drive across the Moors. I was the first to be dropped off. "So how d'ya wanna' do this?" said Clint, as we pulled up outside of 52 Pye Nest Road.
"Let's take mi guitar and amp in first mate and then we'll carry the sheep into the house together."

Once mi music gear was safely stashed in the dining room, Clint and miself headed back to the van to figure out how to get the sheep into the house without any of mi neighbors seeing what we were up to.
It was decided that Clint would take the back end and I would take the front end as Clint was not too comfortable with the horns. Roy kept a good look-out as we struggled up my driveway to the back kitchen door.
"Try not to make any noise Clint. I don't want to wake up Jonna. She'll have a shit-fit if she sees what we're up to."

Although my house was quite big, the kitchen was somewhat narrow so we had to be careful not to dent the fridge and washing machine as we made our way to the cellar door.

"Push the cellar door open Clint, I've got him."

Once the door was opened, the next problem was, getting the sheep down the cellar steps. As we lowered the sheep down the steps, Clint lost his grip and the sheep went tumbling down and came to an abrupt halt as it hit the cellar wall. BAH, BAH!, said the sheep as it lay there in the dark.

"Shut up, ya scungy bastard! You'll wake up the missus."

"Come on Clint, let's get back upstairs and close the door before it wakes up the whole neighborhood."

Back upstairs, Clint said, "Ya know, we can drag it back up the stairs and let it go out on the road if ya don't wanna go through with it."

"That's alright mate, we've come this far now. I might as well finish the job off."

"Do ya need my help anymore Richard cause I've never seen a sheep killed before? I'm not sure I could handle it. I'd probably chuck up mi guts at the sight of blood."

"That's alright Clint, you've done enough. The rest is up to me."

"Alright Richard, I'll get back to the van now."

"No worries Clint. Thanks for ya help."

Once I was back inside the house, I got mi last bottle of Newcastle Brown out of the fridge and rolled miself a smoke. Sitting at the dining room table, I was thinking how I was going to proceed with the

146

butchering of the sheep. The act itself was not going to be a problem for me as I had killed lots of sheep in the Bush. The problem, as I saw it, was there was no drain in the cellar which meant there was nowhere for the blood to run out.

After 10 minutes of sitting at the table, I thought to miself, 'Well, the job's not gonna get done sitting here thinking about it.'

I went into the kitchen drawer to get out mi trusty old butcher's knife. Once I had sharpened it up and put a good edge on it, I went out to the garage for an extension cord so I could rig up a light in the cellar as there wasn't one down there. I took off mi stage clothes and stripped down to mi underwear. I didn't want them to get covered in blood.

Downstairs, in the cellar, as I stood over the sheep. Memories of my life in the Outback came flooding back to me and the first time Dick Skipworth had made me kill a sheep, under the threat of not eating any more mutton until I learned how to do it the correct way. Killing anything had never come easy to me as I always felt for the creature that was about to have its life extinguished.

I turned the sheep over on its side and then parted the wool on its throat area. Then I bent its neck back over my ankle. The next part was the hardest. I cut through the sheep's neck in line with one of its vertebrae and pushed the knife between them, severing the spinal cord in one clean cut. The sheep was now dead and couldn't feel any pain. Its legs tried to kick due to the nerves and the blood pumped out of the large gash. I had temporarily forgotten

147

how much blood a sheep's body holds. Pretty soon, I was up to my ankles in blood.

In the Outback, most farmers will kill a sheep in the paddock so the blood runs into the ground but in my situation, I didn't have that option. The sheep's nerves had now stopped twitching so the next job was to untie its legs. After this was done, I started the skinning process. The whole process normally doesn't take that long but, in this case, I was limited to a small space so I had to make do with the situation. Due to the cellar being small and the house having central heating, it didn't take long for the cellar to get quite warm.

Normally, butchering a sheep outside in an open paddock one doesn't get too much blood on themselves. In my situation, I had blood on my legs and arms. I also had blood on my face from wiping the sweat off my forehead.
I had hung a rope over one of the beams in the cellar and tied the end to the sheep's ham-strings. The next part of the job proved to be really difficult as I had to pull the sheep up high enough so his guts would fall out when I slit his belly open. I pulled the sheep up on the rope and tied the other end of the rope off as best I could. Then I gutted him. I made a small slit in his guts and then inserted two fingers into the slit. I put the point of the knife between my two fingers and carefully ran the knife straight down to his rib cage. SLOSH! His guts fell downwards all over my bare feet due to not enough room to get out of the way. What happened next was the stuff that nightmares are made out of!

22

THE STUFF THAT NIGHTMARES ARE MADE OF

Jonna had woken up and was now standing at the top of the cellar stairs trying to see what I was doing.

"Richard, what you do down there?" she asked

"Nothing." I said from around the corner of the cellar wall.

"Come out so I can see you."

"No, go back to bed Jonna. I'll be up in a short while."

"I no go back to bed till you come out. I like see what you doing."

"Go back to bed. ya won't like what you see."

"No, me get torch so I can see down there!"

Oh fuck! Now what do I do? This the last thing I wanted to happen! Back she came, with the torch and shone it down the stairs. The light from the torch moved around the wall and then settled on the concrete floor that was swimming in blood.

"What all that stuff on floor?"

"It's blood! Now go back to bed."

"No. You tell lies. Is not blood."

"Alright Jonna, have it your way. It's not blood. I'll tell you what it is when I'm finished."

"Finished what? What you doing? Me coming down to see."

"I wouldn't do that if I was you Jonna. You'll freak out!"

"Me no frightened of cellar. Me come down!"

Very slowly, she took a couple of steps down the stairs. At that point there was nothing left for me to do other than show myself at the bottom of the stairs. Stepping out from around the cellar corner, I stood at the bottom of the stairs. By this time, I was covered in blood and had the butcher's knife in my hand.

The moment she saw me, her face went as white as a ghost and for a few seconds she was totally silent. The silence didn't last long before she let out a blood-curdling scream, dropped the torch which rolled down the stairs and disappeared into the blood. Jonna disappeared from sight, still screaming as she took off at high speed. 'Oh fuck! now what do I do? What if she calls the cops, thinking I've killed someone down here!

The only thing left to do was to go back up to the top step and call out to her.

"Jonna, are you alright?"

"I call police Richard! You kill somebody in cellar!"

"Don't be fucking stupid and stop screaming! It's not a person it's a dead sheep!"

"No, you kill someone!"

"I fucking haven't ya stupid bitch! It's a dead sheep we hit with the van on the way home."

"How I know that? You covered in blood!"

"I'm telling ya, it's a dead sheep! I'm skinning it so we can have mutton for our Sunday dinner."

"You promise you no kill someone in cellar?"

"Yeah, alright I promise. It's a dead sheep. Come down and have a look if ya don't believe me."

"No, me no come down there. Me frightened!"

"There's no need to be frightened. It's only a bit of

blood."

"You covered in blood Richard. If it's dead, why is so much blood?"

"Because I had to skin it and take its guts out before we can eat it."

"Me no eat dead sheep."

"Ya fucking eat it when we buy it at the Butcher's shop. It's the same thing except I'm doing it! Just go back to bed. I'll be finished in a bit."

"No, me sleep on couch tonight. Me no want you kill me when I sleep!"

'Chance would be a fine thing.' I thought. "There's nothing to worry about Jonna. Now go to bed."

Once I had settled her down, I went about finishing what I had started. The last thing I needed to do was to put the sheep's guts in its skin, cut the ears off of the head and wrap it up, as best I could.
'I'll pack everything into a big plastic bag in the morning.' I thought. 'I can mop up the blood with the mop and bucket.'

When I finally came up from the cellar, Jonna was sitting on the couch having a cigarette, her fourth one. To lighten things up I said to her, "Ya wanna' be careful smoking too many cigarettes. Those bloody things will kill ya." Jonna never had much of a sense of humor. She said "How I know you not kill me next time we have argument?"

"Ya don't! So be a good lass and you'll live to a ripe old age."

A worried look spread across her face again. She lit up another smoke. "I'm off for a shower so why don't you go back to bed. I won't be long."

"No, me sleep on couch tonight. Me no trust you!"
"Please ya self then. See ya in the morning!"

The following morning, I was sober. As I slowly
woke up, memories of the previous evenings work
came flooding back. 'Oh shit!' I thought. 'What have
I done? Now I'll have a mess and a half to clean up
in the cellar before I can do anything else.'
I got out of bed and checked Anthony's room. He
was still asleep. I carefully closed his bedroom door
so as not to wake him. Once I got downstairs, I
found Jonna asleep on the couch. I carefully snuck
by her on my way to the cellar. I turned on the light
that I had rigged up and walked down the steps.
Before I even got to the bottom, I could see that the
floor was swimming in congealed blood!

 At that point, I decided to go back upstairs and get
mi gumboots out of the closet. 'There is no fucking
way, I'm trampling through that mess without mi
gumboots on.' I thought. 'Why do I have these bright
ideas and why do I have them when I've had too
many beers? Oh well, it's a bit too late to think about
it now. It would have been much better to think
about what I was doing before the event, not after.'

Back down in the cellar, I walked around the corner.
There was the sheep skin sat in a few inches of
blood. The guts were hanging out of the corners
where I'd done my best to tie it up. The Black-Face
sheep that was now a No-Face sheep was hanging
from the beam where I'd left it last night.
All in all, to say that it was butchered under the most
primitive of circumstances, it didn't look too bad. A

153

good wash down with warm water and it would look no different from the meat hanging up in the Butchers shop.

It took me about 2 hours to mop up the blood which I disposed of down the kitchen sink. Once that job was done, I retied the skin that I'd dumped the guts out onto so it could be put into a large, strong plastic bag.

Once everything was as clean as I could get it for now, I put a call into Clint. "Yeah?" said a groggy voice. "Who is it?"

"It's Richard. How are ya mate? Ya don't sound too good."

"I'm not. I'm as sick as a dog and mi mouth tastes like the bottom of a parrot cage. Did we chase a sheep across the Moors last night or was that just a drunken nightmare?"

"No, ya weren't dreaming Clint. That's why I'm calling. What I need from you is 4 large black garbage bags. Have ya got any?"

"No mate but I can get some from our corner store. When d'ya need 'em by?"

"Soon as possible mate. I need to bag up the guts and skin."

"Oh fuck no, ya don't need me to help ya do ya?"

"I sure do mate."

"I don't think I could face something like that this morning without puking mi guts up."

"Sure ya can mate. I've got full confidence in ya Clint and while ya at it, give Roy a call and get him to drive over to my place. We'll need his van to dump the guts somewhere."

"Oh fuck, are ya sure ya can't do it without me

Richard?"

"Positive mate. Ya gotta earn ya meat Clint."

"Alright, give us an hour to get mobile. I'm gonna' need a hair of the dog. Remind me not to have more than 8 pints next gig we do, will ya?"

"I've done that before mate but ya never listen."

"Yeh, yeh, I know. I'm getting off the phone now. I think I'm gonna' puke. See ya soon."

By this time, Jonna was sat up on the couch and Anthony was running around the house playing at cowboys and Indians, of all things.

"Can't you sit down and read a book or something Anthony?"

"Bang! Dead daddy!" he said. "Bang, Bang."

He ran up to Jonna and fired the cap gun in her ear, "Bang, Bang! Dead mommy." Under mi breath, I said, "I wish!"

An hour later, Clint knocked on the kitchen door. When I opened it, he had the plastic bags under one arm and a couple of bottles under the other one.

"Morning Richard, I thought ya might need a liquid breakfast. I know I do. Here's the plastic bags mate. They're the biggest I could get."

"Good on ya Clint. Come in mate."

As soon as Anthony saw Clint, he ran up to him with the cap gun and fired it at him.

"Bang! Clint dead!"

"I wish I was, Anthony." he said as he slumped into a chair.

"Put bloody gun down." said Jonna, who was not in the best of moods.

"No!" said Anthony and then took a couple more

shots at her.

"Put down before me take it from you!"

"No! Anthony not put down. Anthony cowboy!"

"Let him fire the bloody thing Jonna. He'll be out of caps soon. Then we'll get a bit of peace!"

"Can you open one of those beers for me Richard? I'm in desperate need." said Clint.

"No worries mate. Coming up."

"So, where's this bloody sheep Richard? Is it still down in the cellar?"

"It was, the last time I looked Clint. I don't think it's going anywhere now."

"What d'ya need me to do?"

"I'll show ya, as soon as ya finished ya beer."

Normally Clint could down pints of beer like they were going out a' fashion but this morning, he was drinking very slowly.

"Ya not drinking ya beer Clint. Ya not thirsty?"

"It's a stalling tactic. I'm not looking forward to going down those cellar steps."

"Don't worry about it mate. I mopped up all the blood this morning before I called ya otherwise I'd have told ya to come in ya gumboots." Clint's face lost a bit of color and he let go a dry heave.

"Don't tell me that Richard, mi guts are a bit delicate this morning!"

"Tell ya what Clint. We can take a bucket into the cellar with us and if ya need to hurl, you'll have somewhere to hurl it."

"That's very kind of ya Richard but it's not very reassuring."

All though Clint was not in the best of shape, it took me all my time, not to crack up laughing at him.

Once Clint's bottle was empty, I said to him, "Well, are ya ready mate?"

"Ya sure ya can't do it on your own?"

"No way! Come on, don't be such a bloody wuss!"

Clint, very slowly, followed me down the cellar steps.

As soon as he got around the corner of the L-shaped room and saw the sheep hanging up and the pile of skin and guts, he had another dry heave.

"Are ya aright mate? Do ya need a bucket? I can go back upstairs and get one."

"No way! You're not leaving me down here, on mi own, in this house of fucking horrors!"

"Alright Clint, this is how we're gonna do it. We're gonna open up the plastic bag and get on each side of the skin and then maneuver it onto the opening of the bag and then pull the lip of the bag up. With a bit of luck it should slide right in."

"Ya mean we're gonna' have to pick the skin up? It's soaked in blood!"

"Oh for fucks sake Clint, a bit of blood isn't gonna hurt ya. Come on, grab hold of it."

I grabbed a hold of my side of the skin and Clint put 2 finger ends and a thumb of each hand on his side.

"Clint mate, ya never gonna' be able to lift the skin up with ya fingers and thumb! Get a good fucking grip on it. It's not gonna fucking bite ya!"

As Clint grabbed the sheepskin, blood oozed out from between his fingers. That caused him to have another dry heave.

"Are ya ready mate?" I asked.

"Ready."

157

"Alright, after 3!"
"1-2-3, lift!"

As we placed the bundle of skin and guts on top of the plastic bag, one of the corners of the skin fell open where I'd tied it. The sheep's head, minus its ears, rolled out of the bundle onto Clint's foot.
The contents of a fresh bottle of beer flew out of Clint's mouth, at high velocity, all over the bundle of skin and guts.
"Oh, fuck me dead!" said Clint, as he jumped back in fright, at the same time wiping his mouth. "What the fuck is that thing?"
I was now in hysterics as Clint stood there, his back against the cellar wall, looking down at the head.
Once I'd regained a bit of composure, I said between laughs, "It's a sheep's head ya fucking ding-bat! Haven't ya ever seen one before?"
"Yeah, but it was still attached to a body, running around a farmers field. What happened to its fucking ears?"
"They're probably mixed up with its guts inside the skin."
"Why did ya cut its ears off?"
"So no one could recognize it."
"I don't know what ya mean. Is it because all sheep look the same?"
"No mate." I said, still laughing. "They've got a piece clipped out of their ear so the farmer knows who owns them. Every farmer has his own brand."

Once Clint had composed himself somewhat, he said, "I'm sorry about puking all over the skin Richard."

"Don't worry about it Clint. It's only regurgitated beer and I don't hear the sheep complaining."
"The poor fucking bastard. I'm glad I'm not a fucking sheep!"
"Well you'll soon forget about it once it's on ya plate with some roast potatoes and gravy."
"I don't think I'll ever be able to eat meat again, after seeing this!"
"I'll tell ya what Clint, all jokes apart. If people had to kill an animal, skin it and then gut it themselves before they could eat it, vegetables would be in short supply."

For a bit of fun, I said to Clint, "Alright mate, let's finish the job, pick the head up and put it back in the bundle while I tie the corner back up."
"Can't you pick it up Richard? I'll probably puke again, if I have to touch it!" This caused me to start laughing. Between laughs, I said to Clint, "Come on Clint, grab the skin. Don't stand there looking sheepish, it's not gonna' bag itself up."

Eventually, to Clint's relief, the head, skin and guts were all securely tied up and double-bagged so nothing could fall out. Now all we had to do was carry it up the cellar steps, once Roy arrived with the van.

23

SIX MONTHS LATER, A BATTLE ROYAL & THE AFTERMATH!

It was now six months later and Jonna was in the shit again for some reason or other. By this time, I was getting really sick of it. Every time I came home from work, she was sat in the chair staring out of the window in a drugged-up state from taking too many Head-X tablets.

"How are ya Jonna?" I asked as I hung up mi coat. Nothin! No response at all.

"Has Anthony been fed?" Still no response.

Anthony was a very fussy eater. Whenever I asked him if he was hungry, he would always say,

"Anthony no eat. Me want chocolate."

At these times, I would say, "No chocolate until you eat some dinner."

Sometimes I would find chocolate wrappers in the garbage can. That told me he hadn't been fed.

On one particular evening, I decided to put Anthony to bed early as Jonna's behavior was not acceptable any more. I needed to have it out with her. Once I was sure Anthony was asleep, I made my best effort to talk to her. Eventually she spoke, "Give me cigarette. Me need cigarette!"

"Ya know what Jonna, no more cigarettes! I'm not giving ya anymore smokes until ya straighten ya self out and start looking after Anthony properly. I never know whether he's eaten or not. All he seems to want is chocolate which means he must eat a lot of it when I'm at work."

"Give me fucking cigarette Richard!"

"No Jonna, I already told ya, no more cigarettes until ya start acting like a good mother. Ya know what else, I'm not leaving anymore food money with ya 'cause you always buy a bottle of fucking Head-X tablets and eat 8 or 10 of them a day, till they're gone."

"You give me fucking cigarette Richard, you bastard!"

"No Jonna, fuck you! I'm fucking sick of living like this with you. I've had enough! You used to last a week or so before you end up in the shit. Now, it's every three or four days."

"Give me fucking cigarette Richard or you sorry!"

"Fuck you, Jonna. When you fucking grow up and stop acting like a fucking retard, you can have more smokes. Let me tell ya something, when you first came to live with me at Cavendish Buildings, you weren't happy because it was an older cottage. So, what did I do? I bought a really beautiful home for you to live in. You got a new wall-to-wall carpet, a brand-new fridge, washing machine, dryer, expensive curtains upstairs and downstairs, new dining room table and chairs and ya still not fucking happy! Let me tell ya something else, when I first met you, I believed I could make you happy by giving you the good things in life but I was wrong! You're just a miserable cunt! No matter what you get in life, you'll never be fucking happy!"

"Give me fucking cigarette Richard!"

"Fuck you wench!"

With those last three words from me, she got up out of the chair and headed for the kitchen. When she

reappeared, she had the butcher's knife in her hand.
"Give me cigarette or I fucking stab you bastard!"
"Put the knife down and don't be so fucking stupid.
Remember the last time you threatened Anthony
with a knife? The police came!"
"You give me fucking cigarette or not?"
"No Jonna, I already told you, grow up and stop
acting like a retard!"

With that said, she threw the knife at me. The
wooden handle hit my arm and ricocheted off and
hit the wall and landed on the carpet. Without
thinking, I defended myself and gave her a smack in
the chops with the back of my hand. She was
standing next to the couch and although I didn't hit
her hard, she fell backwards onto the couch. It only
took her a few seconds to recover. The first thing she
did was put her hand up to her mouth.
"You fucking cunt bastard!" she said with fire in her
eyes and venom running down her chin. "You
knocked my fucking front tooth out."
"Bullshit! That was only a fucking love tap. If I had
really hit ya, I would have broken ya fucking jaw, ya
crazy bitch!"
"What this then?" she asked as she took her hand
away from her mouth.
"And what this?" she said, as she bent over and
picked up her front tooth off of the carpet.
"It must have been fucking loose to start with bitch.
I didn't hit ya that hard!"
"You fucking knock my front tooth out." she said
again in disbelief.
"Yah well, ya know what? Next time ya throw a
knife at me I'll knock ya fucking head off."

"You fucking bastard!" she said as she rushed straight towards me and grabbed a handful of my long hair. "I fucking kill you!"
Then she started slapping my head with her spare hand and kicking me everywhere she could. She even tried kneeing me in the knackers. When I eventually got my hair free of her hand, long pieces of it were stuck on the front of mi t-shirt. She was now, totally out of control as she kicked, scratched and hit me wherever she could.

I had worked in the boxing troupe on the Showgrounds in the Outback for six months so at any time I could have laid her out with a left hook or a straight right. Even in the midst of her insanity, I couldn't do that to her.
She kept up the fight for about 3 minutes before she finally ran out of wind. I said to her, "What's the matter, too many cigarettes? Out of breath are ya?"
"Fuck you, cunt, bastard!" she screamed so fucking loud, I heard the old woman next door turn her TV up.
"No more fucking for you Bastard! I never give you again!"
"Shove it up ya arse Jonna. It's close enough. Ya know what? Why d'ya think God gave me two hands? It wasn't just for working to feed you, ya ungrateful bitch!"

What surprised me the most about that evening was that Anthony, thankfully, slept through the whole drama.
"What I do now Richard, me have no tooth in the front!"

163

"Put it under ya pillow. The fairies might come and get it and leave ya sixpence, you can buy a couple of fags with that!"

"Fuck you Richard!" she said. that was the last time she spoke to me that evening. Needless to say, she slept on the couch!

Two weeks later, Jonna had still not recovered from her meltdown. It was 7 in the morning on a Monday. I was on the afternoon shift. I got Anthony out of bed, gave him his morning wash and then went through the trauma of getting him to eat something for breakfast. 8 o'clock and Jonna was still not out of bed. I went back upstairs to give her another call.

"Time to get up! You need to watch Anthony. I've got things to do before I go to work."

"Get lost Richard! Me no get up today. You take care of Anthony!"

"Jonna, you need to get up and look after your son!"

"No, me no get up!"

"Alright! If you're not up in 15 minutes, I'll pull all the blankets off the bed. I'm not putting up with your shit anymore. I'm fucking sick of it!"

Half an hour later and still no sign of her getting up. Back upstairs I go.

"Are you getting out of bed today or not?"

"No, go away! Leave me alone!"

"Don't say I didn't warn ya!"

Taking hold of the blankets, I gave a long pull and Jonna was left on the bed with only her nightdress on and still she didn't move.

"Ya getting up now or not?"

"Fuck off! Leave me alone!"
"Next time I have to come upstairs; I'll chuck a bucket of water over ya! Don't think I fucking won't!"

It was now 10 o'clock and she still was not out of bed. I said to myself, 'Fuck it! That's it! I've had a gut full of this crazy bitch! She's getting worse by the day.'

Back up the stairs I go with an empty bucket, intending to put water in it, from the bathroom. First off, I stuck my head around the bedroom door to see if she had moved. There she was, still laid in bed, only this time she was on her back and not on her side.
Walking up to the bed, I said to her, "Last chance! What's it gonna be?" She didn't answer this time so I shook her again as I thought she'd gone back to sleep.
"Last chance!" I said as I shook her again. She didn't speak so I gave her another shake and still no answer or movement. 'Now what the fuck is going on', I thought as I shook her a bit more vigorously. Nothing happened! My first thought was, 'Oh fuck, she's dead!"
I turned my head to her night table and I instantly realized the problem. An empty bottle of Head-X tablets lay on its side with the cap and cotton wool next to it.
"You fucking bitch!" I said out loud. "That bottle was nearly full last night! What the fuck have you done?"
I shook her a few more times but she was dead to

the world. Now I was really worried. I went back downstairs and called 999.

"Which service do you require?" said the voice on the line.

"Can you send an ambulance to 52 Pye Nest Road please."

"What's the emergency?"

"It's mi girlfriend. She's taken a full bottle of Head-X tablets!"

"Is she unconscious or awake?"

"She's out like a light. I shook her but she's not moving."

"Alright sir, I'm sending an ambulance now. It should be there in 15 minutes."

I could hear the ambulance siren going as it sped down Pye Nest Road and stopped in front of the house. I met the ambulance man on the driveway and he said, "Where is she?"

"She's upstairs in bed." I said, as I handed him the empty bottle of tablets. The other ambulance man was taking a foldable stretcher out of the back of the ambulance, then they both took off upstairs. Within minutes they had her strapped to the stretcher and loaded into the back of the ambulance. "Where are you taking her?" I asked.

"Halifax infirmary sir. Would you like to ride with her?"

"No mate, I've got mi son to look after until I can get a baby sitter. Is she gonna' be alright?"

"Well her breathing's very shallow and she's got a faint heartbeat, so there's a good chance she'll make it. Call the infirmary in a couple of hours and they should know something."

"Thanks mate" I said and the ambulance took off at full speed with the siren going. 'What a fucking embarrassment', I thought as I walked up the driveway. Both of mi neighbors, on either side of me, were out watching the whole show.

"Is everything alright?" they asked.

"Yeah, just another drama. No worries."

"Where's mummy gone?" asked Anthony.

"She's gone on holidays for a few days but don't worry, she'll be back home soon."

"Anthony want holiday."

"Not that way ya don't mate. We'll go on holidays soon."

Two hours later, I called the infirmary to check on her and was told that she had her stomach pumped out and was in a stable condition.

"Can I come in to see her?"

"Better leave it till tomorrow. She's still very groggy and resting."

'What the fuck am I going to do now?', I thought as I played with Anthony on the floor with some of his toys. The nurse had told me that young children were not allowed to visit due to the possibility of infections. I would need to see if Clint's wife would watch Anthony tomorrow while I went to visit her.

That evening I'd put Anthony to bed and I had the whole night to think about what I needed to do with my life from this point onwards. This overdose was the last fucking straw. We'd been together just over three years now and instead of her mentally improving, she had only gotten worse. My intention was to call my mother and ask her if she wanted to look after Anthony for a week so I could continue working or I'd have to fake a bad back and get a doctor's note to be off work. That way, I'd at least get the basic wage which was 50% less than I would normally make. That would make paying the mortgage and bills very difficult.

The first fact I had to admit to myself was that doing my best to help Jonna with her ongoing problems was a dismal failure. Now I was free to make a decision as to what needed to be done from this point on. Before long, the right course of action bubbled up to the surface. Sell the house and take her back to Denmark. She'd never really given it a fair go, living in England. She was always talking about how great Denmark was and how much she missed her mother, so she shouldn't put up much resistance. As for myself, I would find some shearing in the South of England. That way, I could get my body back in shape before heading off, back to the Outback.

The next day, I dropped Anthony off at Clint's place. Clint's missus was working but Clint was at home watching his daughter so he had no problem looking after Anthony for a few hours. When I arrived at the infirmary, the receptionist called the Doctor, once I had given her all the information. In a matter of minutes, he arrived at the reception area.
"How's she doing Doc?" I asked.
"Well, we pumped out her stomach and now we've got her on a mild sedative so she can sleep. She became very argumentative once I told her she'd have to stay in the infirmary for a day or so. Do you

have any idea why she took an overdose?"

"She's not happy. She has violent mood swings and has had them ever since we've been together."

"She really needs to see a psychiatrist so she can deal with her issues." said the Doctor.

"She won't agree to it. I've tried to get her to see someone lots of times but she says that there's nothing wrong with her."

"That's highly debatable. One thing's for sure, she's not going to get well on her own. Anyway, we'll be releasing her in 48 hours but if she does it again, we'll have no option but to have her committed for psychiatric evaluation."

"Can't you keep her for a week Doc? To tell ya the truth, I'm sick of it. It's making my life a bloody misery!"

"The law states we're only allowed to keep her here for 48 hours."

"Yeah, but she doesn't understand English law Doc. If you don't tell her then I can tell her she's got to stay for a week."

"Look, I understand your situation but if she insists on leaving then I'll have to sign her out."

"I'm not asking you to lie Doc. What if you just happened to forget to tell her? I'll do the lying so you won't get into trouble."

"It would be good for her to spend a week here, then we could run a series of tests to find out the best way to help her. But again, if she insists on leaving, we can't force her to stay."

"Just do your best Doc. I need some time out miself."

"I've got to get back to the ward now so let me know how you go after you've talked to her."

"Will do Doc and thanks for everything."
When I walked into the ward, Jonna was laid there with a drip in her arm. She looked completely out of it. It was the worst I'd ever seen her. The ward nurse had already told me I could only stay for a few minutes, as Jonna needed to rest. I was tempted to say, she needs a bullet but I resisted the temptation.

As I sat down next to her bed, she opened her eyes. The first thing she said was, "Me want go home! Me want cigarette!"
"Well, for a start, ya can't go home for seven days 'cause ya tried to commit suicide and ya can't smoke in the hospital."
"Me no stay here 7 days. Me go home."
"I just spoke to the Doctor and he said next time you try to commit suicide, they'll put you in a nut house."
"Fuck you Richard, me no fucking crazy!"
"You may not think so but ya not real sane either!"
"Fuck off Richard, me no want you here. You go or I call nurse, have you thrown out!"
"Alright, I'm going. Call me when they release you. I'll come and pick you up."
With that said, I walked out.

24

DEALING WITH BEING A DAD

Once I got home, I called mi mother in Cleethorpes
to ask if she would look after Anthony, so I could go
back to work. I explained to mi mother what
happened. She agreed to look after Anthony for a
week as long as I took him down to her place as she
did not want to come and stay at my house. The last
thing she said to me before she hung up was, "Didn't
I warn you, you'd have nothing but problems with
that lass! But nobody listens to me do they?" I
didn't want to antagonize her, in case she changed
her mind about looking after Anthony, so I just said,
"Yah mum, you were right."

The next day, I caught a train to Cleethorpes. Mi
mother met me at the station. I stayed at her house
for a few hours to make sure Anthony would settle
in alright. When I left, Anthony and mi mother were
getting on like ducks in water. I'd only been back
from mi mothers for three days when the telephone
rang.
"Hello." I said.
"It's me, ya mother."
"How are ya mum? How's Anthony doing?"
"He's alright, but I'm not. You'll have to come down
and pick him up."
"Why? What's wrong?"
"He's too much for me to handle. I can't do anything
with him and he won't listen to a word I say. He
even called me a 'bastard'. Now, I wonder where he
learned that language from? And that's not the only

thing that happened. When I bent over to get something out of the oven, he stuck his hand up my dress and said 'Whee! I've a good mind to send the child welfare to your house. It's not right, swearing and carrying on in front of children at his age."
"Alright mum, settle down. I'll come back down tomorrow to pick him up, but you'd better make the best of your time with him 'cause I'm selling the house and going to live in Denmark."
"What do you mean, you're going to live in Denmark! Ya can't speak the language. How're ya gonna work there?"
"I'm not sure of anything yet mother. We can talk tomorrow when I'm there."

Anthony enjoyed the train-ride back. When we reached Halifax, he didn't want to get off the train and made a bit of a song and dance over it. Once I assured him we could ride on the top deck of the bus, he was in good spirits again.

The following day he was in one of his terror moods. It was the afternoon and I'd just gone outside to the garage to find some casters to screw on the bottom of my speaker cabinet. When I walked back to the kitchen door to open it, the door was locked up tight. I knew immediately what had happened. Anthony had dragged a chair close to the door and pressed the button on the Yale lock and locked me out of the house. 'The little bleeder!' I thought. 'Wait till I get hold of you!' I could see the fuzzy outline of the chair through the frosted glass but no Anthony in sight. I walked around to the front of the house and tried the front door but it was in the same condition

172

as the back one. I was locked out! I looked through the large plate glass picture window and there he was, in the front room.

He had placed the small metal waste-can in the middle of the room and torn up mi morning paper. Flames were coming out of the can as he danced around it in the Indian costume I'd bought him. He had two plastic six-guns in his hands, shouting "Bang Bang!" Then he made a hollering sound like he'd heard the Indians make on the Television.
Knocking on the window, I yelled at him, "Anthony! Open the door!"
He looked straight at me and shouted, "NO!"
"Open the bloody door Anthony!" I shouted back in panic.
Pictures of mi burned-down house and a barbecued kid started to appear in my mind as I shouted to him, through the letter box.
"Open this bloody door or I'll crack ya arse when I get hold of ya!"
"NO!" he yelled back at me.

Looking through the window again, I could see the flames were starting to catch hold of the newspaper as Anthony continued to dance around it. Had it not been such a dangerous situation, I would have seen the funny side of it. He had on a headband with half-a-dozen cheap colored feathers stuck in it, a plastic waist-coat with fringes around the bottom and the plastic fringed pants on, backwards.
"Open the bloody door!"
"NO!" he yelled back.
Once I realized he was not going to relent, I ran to

173

the garage to get a sturdy screw-driver. I ran back to the front of the house where the coal grate was. I prized up the square grate and pushed it over onto the flagstones. I then slid down the coal-chute into the cellar. The coal-chute was covered in coal dust from the years of emptying bags of coal down it.

Needless to say, on the short ride down, I ripped a hole in the arse of mi good jeans. Once I got up the cellar steps and into the kitchen, I grabbed a couple of tea towels out of the cupboard and ran into the front room, just in time to catch him prodding the flames with the ornamental brass poker he'd picked up from the fireplace.
I picked up the can which by this time had become quite hot. Careful not to set mi hair on fire, I raced back to the kitchen. Once the door was unlocked, I moved the chair out of the way, opened the door and tossed the waste can out onto the lawn. The flaming can now had one-foot flames dancing out of it so I got the biggest cooking pot we had, filled it with water and doused out the flames.

Panic had now subsided, so I closed the door and went back into the front-room just in time to catch him trying to play golf with the brass poker and one of the plastic guns.
"Give me that bloody poker!" I said as I took it away from him and put it back on the stand along with the brass-handled hearth brush and pan.
"What the hell are ya playing at? How many times have I told you, no playing with matches!"
"NO!" he yelled at me. "Me play cowboys. Me want fire!"

"I'll give ya fire in a minute mate! I'll set ya arse on fire with mi hand next time ya play with matches!"
"NO!" he yelled again.
"Stop saying NO every time I tell ya to do something!"
He then threw the toy gun at me and said "Piss off bastard!"
Now he was angry. There wasn't much I could do or say so I decided to ignore him. The next thing he did was to throw a shit fit, just like his mother. He threw himself on the carpet and started kicking his legs up and down.
"Stop it Anthony! Behave ya self!"
"NO!" he yelled at me again.
I decided to treat him the same way as I treated his mother when she had a tantrum. I said, "Alright mate, guess who's not getting any more chocolate?" In his mother's case it was cigarettes.
"Me want chocolate!"
"You no get chocolate!"
"Anthony want chocolate."
"Anthony no get chocolate 'cause he's a naughty boy."
"Anthony good boy. Me want chocolate."
"NO, no chocolate!"

Once he realized that I was not going to give in to him like his mother did, he said, "Anthony want go outside."
"Alright, as long as you put ya coat on 'cause it's cold out there."
He'd only been outside for 10 minutes when there was a knock on the front door. When I opened the door, the old lady from next door was standing

there. She didn't look too happy, so I put a warm smile on mi face and said, "Hello love, what can I do for ya?"

"It's about your son! He's laid on his back on your lawn, kicking the stones off of our dividing wall and it looks like it's going to collapse!"

"Oh no, I'm sorry about that love. I'll take care of him right now and I'll repair any damage he's done. Is that alright?"

"Yes, that will be fine as long as you repair the wall. I'm nearly 75. I can't manage to pick up the stones on my side. They're far too heavy for me."

"No worries love. I'll make it as good as new. Again, I apologize for the damage he's done."

"Alright then, thank you."

Mi neighbor headed back to her house and I took off to the back lawn to see what the little bugger was up to this time. I opened the back door a little bit and peered around the wall. Sure enough, the old lady was right. There he was, laid on his back, kicking the dividing wall with both feet.

"Hey!" I said in a loud voice. That made him jump. "What the hell are you doing now? Get away from that bloody wall."

Once he saw me coming towards him, he stood up and said, "Wall fall down."

"The wall didn't fall down. You kicked it down!"

"No, wall fall down. Anthony no kick."

"Don't bloody lie to me Anthony. I'm not as stupid as ya mother. I saw ya kicking it."

"Me want chocolate."

"I already told ya, you're not getting any chocolate

176

and if ya don't stop bloody whinging about chocolate, I'll put ya to bed and you can stay there for the rest of the day."

It took me a couple of hours to repair the wall and it actually looked better than before, once I'd finished. I could have probably done the whole job in an hour had Anthony not insisted on helping me, whilst all the time complaining that someone was naughty for breaking the wall.

25

THE POWER OF NO!

"Me want chocolate! Me want chocolate!"
"How many times do I have to tell you, Anthony,
you are not getting any chocolate!"
"ANTHONY WANT CHOCOLATE!" he said in a
loud, determined voice.
"It will be dinner time soon. Maybe I'll give you
some chocolate after you've eaten all your dinner."

With that said, he yelled at me again, "NO!
ANTHONY WANT CHOCOLATE" This time, I
decided to ignore his demand and headed towards
the small fridge in the kitchen to see what the hell I
was going to cook for him. there were not many
options on the menu so the decision was made for
me. Pork sausages, eggs and brussel sprouts,
embellished with tomato sauce.
'Sounds good to me' I thought, as I cut the snags
apart and stabbed them, quite forcefully, with a
sturdy fork. At this point, I must admit, my cooking
skills had been acquired in the Outback.

It didn't take long before the sausages were spitting
and sizzling away as they drowned in an inch of
Best Refined Lard. Next came the eggs. One for him
and three for me. That should do it.
'Oh shit, I should have put the frozen sprouts on
first. Now the bloody sausages will probably burn a
bit. Oh well, It's the thought that counts I said to
myself.' (which was one of my mother's favourite
sayings.)

Once the half-burned sausage was neatly arranged on the plate and the overcooked egg was put neatly next to it, the brussel sprouts were the crowning glory. A good squirt of ketchup and 'voila, done it!' Another one of my fatherly duties completed!

"Alright Anthony" I yelled. "Come and get your dinner! Sit up at the table mate, time to eat!"
Once he was sat on the chair, he took one look at my gourmet dinner, screwed up his face and said,
"Anthony no hungry. Me want chocolate!"
"Well, you're not getting any chocolate. Maybe I'll give you some for sweets once you've eaten your dinner"
"NO! me not hungry."
With that said, he picked up the fork and started to stab the least burnt piece of sausage that I'd given him.
"Anthony, stop playing with your bloody food and eat it!"
"NO! Me no like!"
"Come on mate." I said in a soft-spoken voice.
"Let's play airplanes."
I put a small piece of the sausage on the fork and flew it around the table a couple of times, at the same time making an airplane noise.
"Zoom, Zoom! Here it comes. Open wide so the airplane can land."
This little game put a smile on his face so he opened his mouth. Without hesitation, I put the sausage in his mouth and pushed it off the end of the fork with my finger.
'Done it!' I thought to myself as I felt a small smile escape from the corners of my mouth.

My little success did not last long as I watched the piece of sausage fly across the table. It did a crash-landing, bounced a couple of times and ended up on my new carpet that I still hadn't finished paying for. My temporary smile disappeared much sooner than it had appeared as I bent down to retrieve the sausage.

"Anthony no like!" he said with a bigger smile than mine.

"Alright Anthony, no more games. Eat your dinner up!"

"NO! me no like!"

By now, I was almost out of patience. I decided to give it one more go before I resorted to a more extreme tactic. My last effort at airplanes was as big a failure as the first one. This time the piece of sausage bounced on the table and landed on my plate.

"That's it!" I said out loud to him. "Are you going to eat that sausage or not?"

"NO!" he yelled at me. "ME NO LIKE! ME WANT CHOCOLATE!"

"You want chocolate Anthony? All right, I'll give you bloody chocolate!"

With that said, I picked up the same piece of sausage, grabbed him by the nose and pinched it real hard. As soon as he yelled out, I put the sausage in his mouth and shoved it down the back of his throat with my finger, to make sure it went down past his clacker. That way he couldn't spit it out again.

No sooner was my arse back on the chair, I heard a

horrifying sound.

"URRRRP!"

I couldn't believe my eyes. There was the same piece of sausage sat on the table. The very same bloody piece! I swear it was smiling at me. The next thing I heard was a voice yelling in my face,

"ME NO LIKE, ME WANT CHOCOLATE!" Then he threw the piece of sausage at me. Then he threw himself off the chair and proceeded to have a full-blown tantrum.

Once the tantrum was over, I said to him, "Are you ready to eat your dinner now?"

His reply was a loud, resounding "NO BASTARD!" With that, he left the dining room, walked into the front room, turned the TV on full volume and sat down two feet away from it.

Many years later, when I was asked to write down the stories of my life, it gave me an opportunity to reflect on the past. It was then that I discovered that my son was a reflection of myself, as a young boy. He was the perfect mirror. Had I known then what I now know, I'm sure I could have done a much better job at fathering.

Why did I get six on the arse with a bamboo cane at school more times than I care to remember? For saying NO! to the educational programming.

"Do as you're told Swindells!"

"NO!"

Why did I get so many thick ears and canings with the curtain rod from my mother?

For saying, "NO!"
"Why can't you be like the boy next door. He's such a lovely lad. He does everything his mother tells him to do!"
"NO! He's a sissy!" was my reply.

Was my father a good role model for raising children? NO.
He survived trench warfare in World War 1 at the age of only 17.
Although his body sat in his armchair, the rest of him was absent.

From my daily observations and what I read and see on the Internet in these, so-called, modern times, I am left wondering about the programming of children out of "NO!" into YES!

I read an article from a children's baseball coach who asked this question,
"What has happened to all of the real men? Where did all of these 'meow men' come from? So afraid to say boo to a goose in case they offend someone."

These are my words of wisdom from 72 years of walking on this beautiful Earth.
"Real men are strong and potent on all levels. They have attained their manhood and are righteously proud of it. They don't project their weaknesses onto others. They don't take shit from anyone! In a nutshell, they stand for Justice which justifiably makes them dangerous!"

Be warned. The next time someone wants you to do

something that goes against your conscience. take a risk and say "NO!"
My way of saying "NO!" is a Universal phrase that everyone understands, FUCK YOU!

26

BACK TO 'BUSINESS AS USUAL

Two days later, the phone rang and the voice on the other end gave me some bad news.

"Your wife is insisting on leaving the infirmary and we need the bed space. You can come and pick her up this afternoon. It's hospital policy not to let her go home on her own."

"Can't ya keep her a bit longer?" I asked. "I'm just getting used to living without her."

"I'm sorry sir. The Doctor said she's been here too long as it is."

"No worries, I'll be there as soon as I can get a sitter for mi son."

I had taken Jonna at her word when she told me to fuck off and not visit her. It had been a week since I had seen her. Apart from looking after Anthony, it had been the most peaceful week I'd had since I met her. Clint's wife wasn't working that day. She said she didn't mind watching Anthony for a couple of hours while I went into Halifax to pick up Jonna.

When I got to the infirmary, the receptionist told me that the doctor would like to talk to me before I took Jonna home.

"How are you Doc?" I said as he walked down the corridor towards me. "How's Jonna?"

"That's what I wanted to talk to you about. She's pretty stable now as we've had her on a mild sedative all week."

"Does that mean the shit's gonna hit the fan once the sedative wears off?"

"It's hard to say but my advice to you is to get her to see a psychiatrist."

"Well, I'll do my best but I can't see that happening. She thinks there's nothing wrong with her."

"Yes well, she's obviously got some problems so do your best to persuade her. I've had a good chat with her myself so maybe this time she'll agree."

"Thanks for keeping her in for a week rather than the 48 hours. I can't tell you how much I appreciate it."

"It's alright, no need for thanks. I just want to see her get well. She's got her whole life in front of her."

"Me too Doc."

"She's waiting in the ward for you but you'll have to sign her out before you take her home."

"I'll do it now before I collect her." I said.

Once I'd signed the papers, I walked down the corridor to the ward where Jonna had been staying. My first impression when I saw her was a good one. She even gave me a great smile as I entered the ward.

"How are you?" I asked.

"Me very good. Me happy. Why you not come and visit me?"

"The last time I was here you told me to fuck off and don't come and visit me."

"I did? Me no remember."

"Oh well, not to worry. I've signed ya out so we can go anytime you're ready."

"Me ready now. Me sick of this place."

"Have you got ya bag packed?"

185

"I pack it early this morning. How is Anthony?"

"He's alright. He's just being a little bugger. I think it's because he misses you."

"Me can't wait to see him. Who look after him now?"

"Clint's wife."

We got off the bus at 52 Pye Nest Road. Once I had Jonna inside the house with the gas fire on, I made sure she was comfortable and had her pack of smokes, I took off to Clint's place to pick up Anthony.

"How's Jonna doing?" asked Clint's missus as she put Anthony's coat on for me.

"She seems great. In fact, it's the best she's ever been since I've known her."

"Maybe her suicide attempt and stay in hospital is what she needed to wake her up. Richard, I still think she needs to see a psychiatrist about her violent mood swings."

"Yeah, I totally agree with you love, but it's not something I can make her do. She has to realize, herself, that she needs help. Anyway, she's home now so we'll see what happens. It's a day-to-day situation. Come on Anthony, let's go and see mummy."

"Mummy on holidays." said Anthony.

"No, mummy's home. Come on, hurry up putting ya shoes on. Let's go see her! Thanks for looking after Anthony, Sue. Say hello to Clint for me."

"Will do Richard, and don't forget, we're here for you anytime you need us."

As soon as we got home, Anthony ran inside to see

Jonna, who was just as happy to see him as he was to see her.

The first week Jonna was home from the hospital, she was fantastic! She seemed really happy and her moods were very balanced. I went back to work the next day. She even got up in the mornings to make me some breakfast. It was like living with a different woman.
Although my relationship with her was never very good, I must admit, I learned a lot of hard lessons along the way. Had I not cared about her as much, it would never have lasted as long as it did. All in all, it happened, therefore it was necessary.

After a couple of weeks of being home, I noticed her moods starting to change and before the month was out, she slipped right back into her old self which was a huge disappointment to me. Once she started taking the Head-X tablets again, I knew it was over. I had no other option but to tell her that I was going to sell the house and take her and Anthony back to Denmark. I broke the news to her as gently as I possibly could but it didn't stop the shit hitting the fan at full force.
"Me no fucking go back Denmark. Me stay here, this my house."
"No Jonna, it's not your house. I pay all the bills and you refuse to work when you could easily have found a good job. You've been complaining about living in England as long as I've known you. How many times have you said you want to live in Denmark with your mother? Well, now you're going to get the chance."

187

"Me no care what you say Richard. Me no moving."
"Jonna, I've had enough of this relationship. I'm done with it! When you first came out of hospital, you were a pleasure to live with and now look at you, you're in the shit again! All you've done for the last three days is sit in the chair popping Head-X pills and staring out the window! I'm having to do everything for Anthony again because you refuse to! So, this matter is settled. I've made my mind up, I'm selling!"
"You fucking bastard Richard! You can't do this. I no move back Denmark."
"Then, I don't know where ya gonna' live once the place is sold. The new people who buy the house won't want you living with them, that's for sure."

The next thing she did was scream and yell at me for being such a bastard and then stormed out of the front room and went upstairs. The last thing I heard was the bedroom door slam so hard it would have wakened the dead.

After work, the next day, I went to see the Estate Agent about selling the house. He said he'd send a valuer out to assess the property so we'd know how much to put it on the market for. I made a time for the inspection when I would not be at work, otherwise, Jonna wouldn't have let the agent in the house.

~27~

SELLING UP AND MOVING ON

The Estate Agent arrived at the house and Jonna,
who was still in the shit, put her outdoor clothes on
and took off for a couple of hours.
"Take Anthony with you." I said before she left.
"He'll enjoy the outside. You could go to the park."
"Fuck you Richard. You selling my house, you
fucking look after him!"

I took the Agent on a guided tour of the house and in
each room he entered information into his note
book. After the tour was over, he gave me a price
that was over double what I was paying for it.
"You honestly think I can get that much for it?" I
said.
"Oh yes sir. Property value has gone through the
roof since you bought this place."
"Do you think it will take long to sell it?"
"Not at all. I've got a couple of families in mind
already. This place is exactly what they're looking
for."
"Well, that's great news. What's the next step?"
"I'll send one of my employees round tomorrow to
put a For Sale sign on your front lawn and take
some photographs of the place. The rest is to up to
me. Don't worry about anything, this place is as
good as sold."

The following day, a bloke from the Estate Agency
hammered a FOR SALE sign into the front lawn
which pissed off Jonna, no end. My life was finally

starting to slowly change, which I'd never thought was possible. I had got used to living this way, even though I didn't want to.

When I got home from work the next day, the first thing I noticed was the For Sale sign was missing from the front lawn. It didn't take long to find it though. It had been thrown under my neighbor's privet fence.

Once inside the house, I said to Jonna "Why d'ya pull out the For Sale sign. It's not going to stop me selling the place."

"You fucking bastard Richard, you sell my house so I pull sign out. You put back. I pull out again."

"No ya won't Jonna, cause this time I'll hammer it into the ground."

It only took me a few minutes to find a sledge hammer that the previous owners had left behind. Back outside on the front lawn, I hammered the sign deep enough so that Jonna couldn't remove it again. 'That'll fix the fucking bitch' I thought as I tried to remove the post myself. After a couple of attempts, I was satisfied that the sign was going nowhere.

"You fucking bastard!" she said as I walked back into the house. "When you at work, I pull sign out again."

"I don't think so. Not this time. Even I can't get it out of the ground now."

"All right, then I burn it out!"

"Ya can try if ya like but if ya start a fire on the front lawn someone will call the cops and the fire brigade and you'll end up in jail or the nut house, so please yourself."

190

I'd only had the house for sale for a month when I got a call from the Estate Agent who said that he had a serious buyer and when was a good time to view it.

"Anytime this week will be good but it'll have to be in the afternoon as I'm on morning shift." I told him. We settled on Friday afternoon. It was now Tuesday.

All week long, I was contemplating the next step I would need to take if this potential buyer agreed to buy the house for the price I had it for sale at. When Friday afternoon arrived, instead of going for a couple of beers with some of the blokes from the Foundry, I rushed home so I could change my clothes and make sure the house was clean and tidy for the potential buyers viewing. I was sat in my chair having a cup of tea and a smoke when a new car stopped in front of the house. The car door opened and a very well-dressed Pakistani stepped out onto the pavement.

The last person I could have ever imagined coming to view the house was a Paki. This was an all-white area and Pakis on Pye Nest road was unheard of. 'Maybe he's just visiting someone.' I thought as I watched him looking at the other houses. It wasn't until he started to walk up my driveway towards the front door that I believed he was coming to view the house.

When I opened the front door, there he was. He stood about 5'6". He had quite dark skin and his hair was slicked back with a lot of hair oil. He wore a dark brown suit, white shirt, mustard-colored tie and brown shiny shoes.

"Can I help you?" I asked and gave him a warm smile.

"Yes, my name is Doctor Sharma. I've come to look at the house you have for sale. Am I too early?"

"No, not at all. Come in please."

The Doctor spoke impeccable English with a slight accent. I asked him a few short questions. Dr. Sharma seemed to like the house as I gave him a guided tour. He especially liked the fact that there was central heating and the big picture window in the living room that I had installed.

"So what do think Dr. Sharma?" I asked him, once the tour was over.

"Very lovely. It's just what I am looking for. I especially like the area. It seems clean and quiet. I'll let your Estate Agent know that I'll be applying for a mortgage to purchase the house. Do you mind if I bring my wife by to see the place, in the next few days?"

"Not at all. You're welcome anytime."

As he got in his car and drove away, one of my next-door neighbors happened to come out of his house as I was walking back up the driveway.

"I see you're selling the place." he said.

"That's right. We're moving to Denmark."

"You're not thinking of selling to a Pakistani are you?"

"I'll be selling to whoever puts the deposit down first."

"But he's a Pakistani!"

"So what? He's a Doctor."

"Well I guess we'll have to sell up soon before the

value of our houses hit rock bottom."

"Why would you say that?"

"Everybody knows as soon as the Pakis' move in, the whole area goes to the dogs! I'm sure the other neighbors won't be too pleased once they find out you're selling to a Wog!"

"If that's the case, why don't you all get together and buy me out, if you're so worried?"

"We don't have that kind of money to spare. Most of us are retired."

"Oh well mate, there is one advantage to having a Pakistani doctor living next door to you."

"Yeah? What might that be?"

"Ya won't have far to go if ya ever get sick. All ya have to do is walk next door."

"I suppose you think that's funny?" he said as he gave me a disgusted looked and walked back inside.

A week later, I got a call from the Estate Agent who said that the Doctor had his loan approved from the Building Society. He asked me when I thought I might be moving out.

"Once everything is signed and there's no danger of him backing out, I'll be gone as soon as it's possible. We're moving overseas so we won't be looking for another house. How long does it usually take to close the deal?"

"I'd say about a month, maybe 5 weeks."

"No worries then. There won't be any delays from my end, I can assure you of that."

"Who that?" asked Jonna, once I got off the phone.

"The Estate Agent. He said the Pakistani Doctor's mortgage application has been approved, so it's only a matter of weeks now and you'll be back home with your mother."

Once Jonna had tried to remove the For Sale sign again and failed, she had no other option but to accept the fact I was taking her back home to Denmark.

"Me no happy leaving my house!"

"You've never been happy since I've known you. Don't you remember what you said when we lived in Cavendish Buildings? You said that if I bought a better house to live in you'd be much happier, remember? Things don't make people happy. Some people have much less than you have been given over the last few years and they're happy. You think living in Denmark again will make you happy? As soon as the novelty wears off, you'll be in the shit again."

"Fuck off Richard." she said as she lit up another smoke. "I don't like you anymore."

"Did you ever?" I asked.

That was the end of that stimulating bit of conversation.

The next five weeks seemed to fly past. I had given the band a month's notice so they could find someone to replace me. No one was happy that I was quitting because they would find it hard to replace me as I played trumpet, guitar and I also sang really well. I gave notice at the Foundry. They were also not happy to see me go as I was a top wage earner and made lots of money for them.

The Estate Agent had called me, one last time, to let me know that the profit I'd made from selling the house had been deposited in my account and I could start using it any time I liked. Everyone who had been involved in the sale of the property had been paid. Whatever was left over was mine to do with as I saw fit.

The first thing I did was to go into Halifax and withdraw the money from my account which was a tidy sum. I closed the account as there was no way I'd be needing it anymore. As far as I was concerned, living in England, on a permanent basis, was now over for me.

28

RETURNING JONNA TO HER MOTHER

I found a Travel Agent and booked the tickets to Denmark. The Ferry left from Harwich three times a week so there were no worries there. Before long, I walked out of the office with train tickets and ferry tickets from Sowerby Bridge Station to Arhus Denmark.

The day before we were due to be out of the house, I took Anthony to Ripponden to see his Grandad. I asked Jonna if she wanted to come with us but she said, "No, why I want to see that old man? You and him are just the same."

We spent an hour with mi dad who was sorry to see me go. He had a difficult time expressing it. Anthony didn't really understand what was happening. He just ran around mi dad's house opening doors and cupboards to see what mischief he could get into.

"When are you leaving?" asked mi dad.

"Tomorrow morning, we get a train from Sowerby Bridge to London, another train to Harwich, then an overnight ferry to Denmark."

"What are ya gonna do then, live there?"

"I don't know yet dad. It depends how happy Jonna is, living in her own country."

"That wench of yours is the same as ya bloody mother. She'll never be happy, no matter what you do for her."

"Yeah, ya probably right dad but I promised miself when I first met her that if it didn't work out I'd make sure she got back to Denmark. She wouldn't survive in England on her own."

"If I was you lad, I'd dump the cow on her mother's doorstep and not look back. That bloody wench has brought you nowt but misery since the first day you met her."

"Yeah, well we probably wouldn't have stayed together if I hadn't got her pregnant."

"That's what happens when a man's brains are in the head of his dick instead of the head on his shoulders. Ask ya old dad. He's been through the mill with that bloody mother of yours."

"I think I only stayed with her in the beginning because she was pregnant and also, I was a bit lonely."

"Better be bloody lonely than miserable lad. I wouldn't have another bloody wench in my life, even if ya paid me."

"Do you ever get lonely dad, after all these years of living on ya own?"

"Do I buggery, lad. I've got miself to talk to and if I get sick of that I can always talk to the Television. At least that doesn't answer me back!"

After spending some time with mi dad, I said, "Well dad, I'd best be on mi way. I got a few last minute jobs to do before tomorrow."

"Aye, alright lad. Thanks for coming to see yer old dad before ya leave."

"No worries dad. Come on Anthony, get your coat on, we're off."

"No! Me stay here."

"Ya can't stay here mate and besides, we're going on holidays tomorrow."

Mi dad saw us to the door and I gave him a hug and said, "I'll see ya next time I come back to England." "Aye well, I'll probably be bloody dead by then. Ya can visit me in Ripponden graveyard. Don't forget lad, dump that bloody wench off at her mother's place. She had her, let her look after the cow!"

Finally, the last day had come. Everything that was going had been packed into suitcases or sold. Whatever was staying was left behind. The taxi pulled into the driveway right on time and the driver helped me load up four large suitcases. I took one last look at 52 Pye Nest Road and thanked it for the roof it had provided over our heads for the last 18 months and also for the large amount of money I had made out of it due to the sky-rocketing housing market.

"So, Sowerby Bridge Station." said the driver. "Yeah, that's right." I said as I climbed into the front seat. "Going on holidays are ya then?" "Yeah, a permanent holiday mate, we're leaving the country." "Oh, lucky you. You're getting out of the country at the right time. This place is going to the dogs, what with all the strikes and everything. Me and the missus have been talking about selling up and going out to New Zealand to live. She's got a sister living out there and she want us to emigrate." "Do it mate, you won't be sorry. It's a great place. I'm an Aussie citizen so I can work over there anytime I like. There's plenty of work and the people are warm and friendly, especially the Maoris." "Funny you should say that, the wife's sister is

198

married to a Maori bloke. She says the same thing."

It didn't take long to reach the station as it was a short drive. The driver helped me out with unloading the suitcases. I thanked him and gave him a reasonable tip and wished him well. I found a trolley and loaded the cases onto it and then we made our way to the platform where we'd catch the train to London. I had to keep a good eye on Anthony as all he wanted to do was climb down onto the railway tracks.

"How are ya Jonna?" I asked as she stood there on the platform, bundled up against the cold wind.
"Me alright."
"Ya happy now that you're going home? You'll be at ya mothers' place by this time tomorrow."
"Me like stay in my house but you not let me. You sell it!"
"Yeah, that's right. I sold it for a very good reason. All you had to do was go to work like you promised and we could have stayed there."
"Me no like work."
"So what d'ya think we're going to do in Denmark for money? I can't speak the language which means you'll have to work."
"I get a job with my mother cleaning railway carriages at Aarhus station."
"What if there are no jobs available?"
"I go to Social Security. they give money for living on and pay for good apartment close to my mother. Maybe you get job on docks Richard. Plenty of foreigners work on the docks in Aarhus."
"Yeah, maybe, but I don't speak the language."

199

"Everybody speak English in Denmark. We learn at school."
"So how come you didn't speak English very good when I first met you?"
"Me no like school so me no go."

The train ride to London was quite pleasant. Anthony had a grand old time looking out of the windows and running up and down the carriage until he finally wore himself out and went to sleep which was a blessing for me.

Sad to say, I always felt that Anthony had some slight brain damage due to the fact of all the pills his mother took while she was pregnant. These days, children like Anthony are called Hyper-active and given drugs to quieten them down. He also had a learning disability, later on in his life. When he went to school in Denmark he had to be placed in a special school for children with the same problems.

The train arrived at Kings Cross station on time. The next leg of our journey was a train ride to Harwich where we would board the overnight ferry to Esberg Denmark. The cabin I had booked was very comfortable. It had two single beds so Anthony would have to sleep with Jonna, which she didn't mind.

The first shock I got on the ferry was when we went to the cafeteria for a meal. The prices in comparison to England were at least three times higher. I could have bought miself a good meal at a restaurant in Halifax for the price of a ham and cheese sandwich.

'Oh well', I thought. 'It's just as well I'm not broke.'

Being on the ferry with Anthony was an absolute nightmare as he was so excited to see the ocean. At one point I caught him, just in time, as he was in the process of climbing through the railings that ran around the outside of the ferry. I only had to take my eyes off him for a second and he was gone, getting into some sort of mischief or other. Like it or not, I would have to restrict his movements.

Back at our cabin, I found a piece of rope that I'd used to tie some things to one of our bags. Once I'd got the knots undone, I made my way back upstairs to where Jonna was supposed to be watching him. When I reached the deck, there was Jonna sat in a deck chair smoking a fag and staring out the window at the waves.
"Where's Anthony?"
"He go looking for you. Me think you had him."
"Are you fucking kidding me? I told you to watch him! He's probably jumped overboard by now! You go to the back of the ferry and I'll go to the front. I'll meet ya back here."

Jonna was now out of her daydream and was quite worried as she took off to look for him. I walked to the front of the boat. After a couple of minutes, I spotted him talking to a group of young Danish people.
"Anthony, come here." I said as I reached their table.
"No! Anthony no come."

One of the young teenagers, who had been talking to Anthony, started to laugh when he said 'No'. Then she said to me, with a strong Danish accent,

"He's so funny. He's been telling us he's going to see his grandma in Denmark."

"Yeah, he is, but it's not so funny looking after him. He's never been on a ferry before. I just caught him trying to climb through the railing."

"Oh, that's not good."

"No it's not. Like it or not, I'm gonna' tie him to mi belt with this piece of rope so if you hear some screaming and yelling, you'll know what it's about."

"Better that than falling off the boat." said one of the other girls.

"Bye Anthony." said the group as they gave Anthony a little wave.

"No!" said Anthony as he refused to wave back.

Once we were out of ear shot, I said to Anthony, "That's it for you mate. You're done running around on your own. If you fall in the ocean you'll be shark tucker. You'll be as dead as a maggot!"

"No, me no dead. Anthony like run around."

"Well, you can tell Anthony for me, he's gonna be tied to my belt from now on."

Once we got back to where Jonna was waiting for us, she yelled at him and smacked his leg. Anthony started to cry, then he started to shout at her just like she would shout at me when she couldn't get her own way.

Next day, around 1 o'clock, the Ferry docked at Esberg. After we got our luggage, we made our way through customs with no problems at all. Standing at the platform, waiting for the train to Aarhus, was the worst part of the trip as the weather was freezing cold. I thought England was a cold place but Denmark took the cake. It was so cold that I had to open one of the cases and find three more jumpers before we froze to death.

"I thought you said Denmark was a great place Jonna. It's bloody freezing here. I hope it's warmer in Aarhus."

"Is winter so is cold. Is same in England."

"It wasn't this cold when we left Pye Nest. January and February are usually the coldest."

After a 45 minute wait, the train to Aarhus finally arrived. I, for one, was as happy as a pig in shit sitting in a heated carriage. Compared to how far we had traveled over the last 18 hours, the journey from Esberg to Aarhus was over before I knew it.

Jonna had called her mother before we left and given her our travel schedule. If all went according to plan, her step-father would be waiting at the station for us, in his car, to take us on the last leg of the trip. Aarhus was the last stop for the train. I would have plenty of time to get our four heavy suitcases off and onto the platform.

Whilst I was in the process of removing our cases, Jonna walked up to an older man and gave him a hug. As soon as they finished hugging, the man picked up Anthony and greeted him. Anthony wasn't too keen on a stranger picking him up so he hit him in the face. As I watched, Jonna and the man had a good laugh and then walked towards me and the cases.

29

MEETING THE FAMILY

"Hello, me Jens." said the man. "I Jonna's step-far."
"My name's Richard, good to meet ya mate."
Jens English was terrible as he had not taken
English lessons at school. It was probably not
compulsory in his day. He took off to find a trolley
as the cases were too heavy to carry any distance.
"That Jens. He my mother's boyfriend. He treat my
mother like Queen but my mother treat him like shit
most of the time."
'That sounds familiar.' I thought to myself. I decided
not to voice that thought out loud.

Once we all in the car with two cases in the boot and
two on the back seat, we drove out to a place in the
country called Tilst.
On the drive to Jonna's mothers house, Jens and
Jonna chatted away in Danish. Each time I asked her
to translate for me, she refused to and said,
"It nothing. We talking about family."
I sat in the car, wondering what it was going to be
like living with a family that barely spoke any
English. It wasn't looking too positive.
We got to the apartment, Jonna introduced Anthony
and myself to her family. Her mother said something
to me in Danish and then had a nervous laugh to
herself as she didn't speak a word of English. Then I
met one of her brothers, who's hair was as long as
mine. He was 15 years old and spoke quite good
English.
I found out later that her other brother was in a

Remand home for stealing. He apparently was a kleptomaniac. There was a sister, Ina, who was about 14 and done up with full make-up. She barely spoke any English. Yetta, another sister, who was 9, was cross-eyed and wore strong bifocal glasses. By the way she acted, she was obviously retarded. Another sister, Hanna, was married and lived a couple of blocks away in the same apartment complex.

"Yetta got brain damage. Not listen if she say something to you." said Jonna.

"She can't speak English, so how would I know what she's saying"I said.

Jonna's father, who lived in Aarhus, I later found out was a sort of porn aficionado. He used to trade porn books with his friends.

That about covers the whole family.

As I sat at the table with them smoking cigarettes and drinking strong black coffee, listening to them talking and laughing away in Danish, I was not able to understand a word of what was being said.

Every now and then Jonna would tell me a bit about what their conversation was about but it was all out of context so it didn't make much sense. At these times I would say, "Oh really or that's lovely."

Anthony was having a good time playing on the polished wooden floor with Jonna's retarded sister Yetta. Everything was going well for quite a while until Yetta took one of her possessions back from Anthony, who got the shits and smacked her in the nose which sent her bifocals skidding across the floor. As luck would have it, they didn't break. When Yetta retrieved her glasses, she checked them out and put them on. She could see Anthony, who was sitting in the same place, and walked over to him and smacked him in the head. Anthony, who was not used to playing with other children and had no concept of sharing, rolled over and bit Yetta on the leg, who in turn let out a loud shriek and then came running across the room to her mother who couldn't care less. When Yetta told her mother what happened, she just sat there and had a good laugh.

After a while of sitting at the kitchen table, I moved to a more comfortable chair. After all, I couldn't understand any of the conversation so I figured I wouldn't be missed. I'd only been sat there for 5 minutes when the 14 year old sister, Ina, who was well-endowed with breasts and had a low cut top on, decided she was going to get to know me better. She walked over to my chair, sat herself down on my knee and put her arm around my shoulder and flashed me a 'come-on' smile and bent forwards so I could get a good eyeful of her perky breasts.
'What the fuck is going on now?' I thought, as I returned her smile. 'This 14 year old school girl is sitting on my knee flashing, her tits at me!'

A few seconds later, Jonna saw what was happening and raced across the room. She grabbed Ina by the hair and dragged her off my knee. All hell broke loose! The pair of them stood toe-to-toe, screaming at each other in Danish. Before long, even Esther, the mother, joined in the huge drama.

I asked Fin, the brother, what was happening and why Ina had come and sat on my knee.

"She's trying to steal you away from Jonna. Ina has always been jealous of Jonna's boyfriends. This is not the first time it's happened."

"How's that possible Finn? Jonna's been away from home for 4 years? Ina would have only been 10 years old then."

"What can I tell you. Ina has always been jealous of Jonna."

We had been living at Jonna's mothers place for a month now. Instead of Jonna becoming happier because she was living in her own country, she very quickly became worse. Every time I mentioned getting our own apartment, she flatly refused, saying she was happy where she was. Neither of us were working so money was constantly going out with nothing coming in.

Three times a week I would catch a bus into Aarhus and walk down to the docks looking for day laboring. As soon as the hiring boss found out I didn't speak Danish he said, "Foreigners to the back of the line!" which I totally understood.

It didn't take long before Jonna started to talk about going out to night clubs. When I said, "No way! We haven't even found work yet." the shit hit the fan. Being back in Denmark changed Jonna's whole personality. She seemed to imagine she was a single woman again and started to act that way. Every time I disapproved of something she wanted to do; she would tell me to get fucked.

"You no tell me what to do anymore!"

~30~

THIS IS IT! I'VE HAD ENOUGH! I'M OFF!

The whole situation had become intolerable for me so I decided to call a shearing contractor I knew of, who lived in Dorset England. When the phone was picked up at the other end, a voice with a thick Scottish accent said,

"Billy Kinghorn here, can I help you?"

"Yeah Bill, my name's Yorky. I shore with your brother a few years back in Cheviot, New Zealand. Ya got any shearing going on?"

"No Yorky, not at the moment. It's a bit early. We don't start up for another six weeks but I can give ya plenty of work lambing if that would suit ya. Have ya done any lambing before?"

"Yeah, I've done a bit in the Outback of Australia but I'm no expert."

"That doesn't really matter 'cause I've got my resident Shepherd who's worked with me for years. He can show ya the ropes. The only thing ya may not like is it's a 24 hour job. Ya take turns sleeping for a few hours at a time."

"That sounds alright to me Bill. When could I start?"

"How about yesterday?" he said and had a bit of a laugh to himself.

"I'm living in Denmark at the moment but I can be there in 3 or 4 days."

"That would help me out tremendously Yorky. I'm glad ya called. By the way, I'm paying fifty quid a day, which is top money, 'cause it's a really busy time and laborers are hard to find."

"Sounds good to me Bill. I'll give ya a ring and let ya know when I'm on mi way."
"So, ya shore with Jerry in Cheviot eh? I'm planning on going over there miself next season."
"Good on ya mate. I'll git ya a pen with the contractor I work with. He's got a big run and he's a decent bloke to shear for." I said.
"I'll take ya up on that Yorky. I gotta' go now mate. Give us a ring when ya get to Wareham Station and I'll pick ya up, if ya need me to."
"No worries Bill, see ya soon."

I couldn't say in words how I felt after I'd put the phone down. This was the first time in four years talking to someone who spoke the same language as I did.
All that from one simple phone call!

Jonna and Anthony had gone into Aarhus, shopping for the day with her mother and older sister. I had lots of time to contemplate how I was going to break my good news to her.
'50 quid a day! I haven't made money like that since I took a break from shearing and starting in a few days. I can't believe my luck.', I thought.

Jonna, her mother and Anthony, returned home from shopping in the late afternoon loaded down with shopping bags.
"How are ya Jonna?" I asked as she dumped all the bags on our bed.
"Me happy. My mother buy me and Anthony lots of new clothes and we go to good restaurant for something to eat."

209

"Well that's great. I'm happy for you."

"I meet two of my old girlfriends at restaurant and I go to a disco with them tonight."

"No worries. I'll come with you."

"No Richard, I go myself. You no come."

"And who do you think is going to look after Anthony while you're out drinking and dancing?"

"You look after him. If you no like, my mother take care of him."

"What if I tell you, you can't go?"

"I no care what you say anymore Richard. I back in Denmark so I do what I want!"

"Is that so? Well let me tell you something cunt face, I made a phone call today to a shearing contractor in England and I can start work with him anytime I like."

"You leave me and go back England to work?"

"Yeah, I'm thinking about it."

"You never leave me Richard. I no care if you do."

"Really Jonna? If that's the case, I'll go into Aarhus tomorrow and buy a ticket for the Ferry."

"Me no care! Me go out and have fun with my friends tonight."

"You think I'm joking but I'm not."

"Me no care. You do what you want!"

She started to remove the new clothes from the bags and held them up to herself in the full-length mirror like she never had a care in the world.

That evening, she took a shower, did her hair, applied full make-up and then put on one of the new short dresses her mother had bought her and then rang for a Taxi.

"Where ya getting all this money from for Taxis and

210

Discos?"

"My mother give me money. I pay her back when I start work."

"And when will that be?"

"When I feel like it."

The Taxi arrived a while later. Jonna put on her coat, said goodnight to Anthony and that was the last I saw of her till she arrived home drunk, at 6 in the morning. I didn't have to think twice about taking a bus to Aarhus to buy a Ferry ticket. As soon as I'd given Anthony some breakfast, I walked out to the road to wait for the bus. The Ferry, back to Harrich, was due to sail in two days. I paid for a ticket to sleep on the deck in a deck chair. I would be on my own this trip so I didn't need the creature comforts of a cabin. Lots of young people took the Ferry without booking a cabin.

The following evening, Jonna decided to go out Disco dancing again. This time I didn't try to stop her. In fact, I told her to have fun. My change of attitude confused her. She had no idea at all what my plans were, as she was so wrapped up in her new-found life.

"Why you no angry I go out tonight Richard?"

"What's the use of being angry with you? It's not going to make you change your mind is it?"

"No. I live England with you four years and no go out."

"That's not true. I took you on gigs with me when I was in the band but most of the time you didn't want to go."

"Why I want to go those old people clubs and listen

211

to that shitty music you played. Me like modern disco music and Danish beer."

"If that makes you happy Jonna, who am I to stop you."

"I more happy here in Denmark. I have Anthony, my family and my girlfriends. I no leave Denmark again." With that said, she got ready to go out on the town, partying with her girlfriends.

That evening, when Anthony and the rest of the family had gone to bed, I packed a bag with enough clothes to get me through the first week in England. I would buy some warm working clothes when I got to Bill Kinghorn's place.

I didn't sleep much that night as I didn't want to miss the earl bus into Aarhus. I also didn't want Jonna to catch me asleep when she got home, drunk again. It was about 4:30 in the morning when she finally walked into the bedroom.

"How are ya Jonna?" I said with a decent smile on my face. "D'ya have a good time?"

"Richard, you wait up for me?" she said in a drunken slur.

"Yeah, sure. I couldn't sleep."

She was more drunk this morning than she had been the previous morning. She said, "Me love you Richard. You good man. You let me do what I want now."

"Yeah, me good man. Now you can go out partying every night and come home whenever you like."

"You stay home and look after Anthony like good father." she said.

"Why don't you go to bed before you fall over and

hurt yourself?"

"Yes, me very drunk Richard. My friends all drunk too!"

"I'm sure Jonna."

"I get undressed and go to bed now. You like some pussy pussy? Me feel like fucking."

"Yeah sure Jonna, I thought you'd never ask."

I watched her undress and throw her new dress over the back of a chair. She took off her bra and panties and tossed them in the general direction of the chair but they landed on the floor. Then she fell backwards on the bed and said, "Come on then, take off your clothes."

Inside, I was fuming, fucking angry that the stupid Danish cunt thought she could talk to me anyway she wanted and then tell me to fuck off when I told her to do something for her own good or Anthony's welfare but I never said a fucking word. I certainly didn't bother with any foreplay in case she flaked out before we got to the main part.

All the time I was fucking her, I kept seeing pictures of the last 4 years of living with her. All the times I had done good things for her like setting her up in a beautiful house with the best of furniture, wall to wall expensive carpets that I had to work my arse off to pay for. All the times I had to look after Anthony when she refused to because she had the shits or was too out of it on pills to care.

'You stupid dumb cunt.' I thought as I finished. I wiped mi dick on her side of the sheets. 'You think I'm gonna put up with your fucking bullshit and let some sick fuck, like you, lay the law down to me.', I thought to miself.

"Oh, that was lovely Richard. Me go to sleep now. Make sure you give Anthony his breakfast. Wake me this afternoon. Maybe I go out for while tonight."

"No worries love. I'll run you a lovely hot bath when you get up." I said.

She rolled over and pulled up the blankets to make herself comfortable. The last thing I said to her was, "Oh, I almost forgot to tell ya Jonna. I'm leaving for England this morning."

"You no leave me Richard. You joking. You love me too much."

"I'm leaving you some of the money I made out of selling the house and make sure you look after Anthony."

"Me no talk now, me tired. You tell me again when I wake up."

When I went into Anthony's room to tell him I was leaving, he was sitting up in his bed playing with one of his toys. I didn't say much to him as I didn't want to cry. I didn't want him to cry or it would have hurt my heart too much.

"Hey Anthony, Daddy's leaving now to go to work in England."

I'm not sure how much he understood about what I said. He looked straight into my eyes and said, "Daddy coming home?" I now had a big lump in my throat the size of a golf ball. Once I'd succeeded in swallowing it back down, I said, "Yes Anthony, Daddy coming back soon, alright?"

All he said was, "Farewell Far" which in English meant, "Bye Dad."

I took my bag out of the cupboard where I'd stashed it and was in the process of walking out the door when Jonna's mother, Ester, walked out of her bedroom. When she saw the travel bag, she said, in Danish, "You leaving?"

"Yes." I said in Danish.

"You good man Richard." she said. "Jonna crazy woman. You no come back?"

"No Ester, me no come back. Thanks for having me here."

She must have understood what I said because tears ran down her cheeks and she put her arms around me and said, "Crazy, crazy Jonna, same her father. Me no blame you."

I picked up my bag to leave and swallowed another golf ball size lump as I walked down the two flights of stairs, then off to the bus stop.

From the time I walked out of Ester's house and the four-year relationship with Jonna, my happiness increased by the minute. The most difficult thing I had ever done in my life, up to that point, was to leave Anthony in Denmark with his mother. There was no way in hell, I could continue to live with her as she had no respect for me at all. I also realized that had I of stayed there, against my better judgement, I would've ended up strangling the bitch, to put her out of her misery. I'd come close to doing just that a few times before, in England. The thought of sitting behind bars for years on end always stopped me doing it.

As I sat on the bus into town, I was contemplating

all the things that had happened since I met Jonna at the Triangle Pub. The arguing and fighting that Anthony had been subjected to over the short span of his life was no longer acceptable to me. My thinking was, with me out of the picture, Jonna would have no one to run her shit on and she'd have to take care of her wounded emotions and her completely unstable mind.

Before I got off the bus in Aarhus, I thought to myself, 'Why are you still thinking about that bitch? You've only been gone for 40 minutes and you've already wasted 39 of them thinking about her! The problem with you, Yorky mate, is misplaced kindness. You care too much for people who don't care enough about themselves. Take it as one of life's hard-earned lessons and forget about her.'

As I was leaving Denmark through the customs, the last thing the Officer said to me was, "I hope you enjoyed your stay? Come and visit us again."
"Thanks mate." I said and walked out of Denmark onto the Ferry.

EPILOGUE

Years after I left my ex-wife and son in Denmark, I received a letter, whilst living in India that my ex-wife had been murdered and my son placed in a special school. At this point, I decided the right thing to do would be to return to Denmark and find out what was happening to him. I had been back two or three times, over the years, to see him.

On one previous occasion, I met her current boyfriend Mario. He was a hot-blooded Italian. It was obvious to me, in our conversation, that he was jealous of me and thought that I had designs on taking her back.

"Mario, I can assure you 100% I have no interest whatsoever in Jonna! She caused me four years of absolute grief and misery! I am here, wholly and solely to see my son! She is your problem now mate and I wish you the best of luck! You're going to need it, a lot of it! A word of advice, if you're willing to take if. She's doing her best, in my company to make you jealous. Don't buy it mate. She's a very manipulative woman. In her own stupid way, she's quite dangerous!"

He was a bit more at ease after our conversation.

Anthony was 10 years old at the time of his mother's murder. I asked him if he wanted to come and live with me until he was old enough to make his own decisions but he declined. It was obviously a difficult decision for a young boy to make. I left him at the special school as I knew I would not be able to look after him and give him the care and education he was receiving there, due to my lifestyle.

It was a very high-profile court case in Aarhus, Denmark. Mario was convicted of murdering her by strangulation and sentenced to life in jail. He committed suicide after a few months of incarceration. At his trial, my ex-wife's family members presented her as being of saintly character and a good mother when in fact, she was a well-known prostitute and had been for many years. I still feel for Mario's family, all these years later.

Had the court read my story, the outcome would have been different. They would have seen a picture of a history of abuse of myself and of Anthony.

Lightning Source UK Ltd.
Milton Keynes UK
UKHW021129190622
404636UK00004B/80